Contents

Introduction

Welcome to the *Cambridge IGCSE™ First Language English Workbook*. This book is designed to complement the fourth edition of the Student's Book and to provide additional exercises to help you develop and practise the skills and concepts you are learning during your course.

Links to the relevant chapters in the Student's Book can be found in the contents list as well as at the start of each section. Each section contains a range of practice exercises with questions that follow the style of those from Papers 1 and 2 of the Cambridge examination. These will help you develop your skills and practise applying them to a range of questions, and also help you in your preparation for examination by becoming familiar with the types of questions. Support for Coursework and the Speaking and Listening Test can be found in the Student's Book.

Reading

Short-answer comprehension questions

The exercises that follow will help you develop your skills in active reading, comprehension and understanding of writer's effects. Remember to concentrate on the following points:

- Read both the passage and the questions carefully before you start to answer the questions.

- Underline or highlight the key words in each question.

- When answering the questions, use your own words whenever possible in order to show your understanding of what you have read.

- The marks shown at the end of each question can be an indication of how many points you should make in your answer. For example, if there are 2 marks available for the question, then you should give two distinct points in your answer.

Exercise 1

Read carefully the following extract from an article about the North-west Passage by Sarah Barrell. Then answer the questions which follow, using your own words as far as possible.

The North-west Passage: A 21st-century expedition

Sarah Barrell

A cruise, led by Inuit people, follows the early explorers around the Canadian Arctic in waters that are still largely uncharted. Sarah Barrell went aboard.

Summer in the Arctic and dust, not snow, covers the ground. In Gjoa Haven, an Inuit settlement on King William, an island in the heart of the North-west Passage, there's dust on the seats of skidoos. Dust, too, on the coats of the scrappy sled dogs that are tethered in long lines waiting for winter and starter's orders.

About them, teenagers charge around on battered all-terrain vehicles, kicking up more dust, making the most of the light evenings and the comparatively balmy 10 °C temperatures. It's hard to imagine amid all this, with the sun shooting in laser-bright arcs off the town's tin-roofed houses, that somewhere in or around this island, Sir John Franklin, Britain's most intrepid 19th-century Arctic explorer, met a dark and icy end trying to discover the fabled North-west Passage.

→

He vanished more than a century and a half ago, but the fever to find the remains of Franklin's expedition still runs high in the remote Canadian Arctic, some 5000 kilometres from British shores. Earlier this summer, Canadian authorities unveiled the wreck of HMS *Investigator*, one of the many doomed 19th-century rescue ships sent in search of Franklin's expedition. Then, just last week in the town of Gjoa Haven itself, archaeologists unearthed what could be the Holy Grail of Arctic exploration history. At the behest of local brothers Wally and Andrew Porter, a box was excavated containing, the Porters claim, long sought-after records from the ill-fated Franklin expedition that might reveal its final whereabouts.

He was old, overweight and his ships spectacularly over-burdened when Franklin left for his third Arctic expedition in 1845. The British Admiralty brushed this aside as the fervour to conquer the North-west Passage once again reached a peak. There was prize money at stake (£20 000 [USD 28 000] offered by the British crown) for anyone who could navigate the elusive, icy waterway connecting the Atlantic and Pacific oceans. But beyond this, there was the chance to forge crucial northern trade links between Europe and the Orient, one that would open up a new route to the spice lands and, in addition, avoid stormy sailings around Cape Horn. But was Franklin the man to fly Britain's flag into the uncharted north?

Probably not, given that he had survived his first expedition charting Canada's Arctic coast by eating his own boots and being rescued by Native Americans. There was much that European explorers could learn from the three centuries of sailors who had battled to find a northerly route connecting the Atlantic and Pacific – in short, to travel light and use local expertise. Instead, highlighting the egotism of the time, Franklin's expedition sailed out of London laden with chests of fine china, dead-weight sledges and canned food that would later finish them off with lead-poisoning. After three winters trapped in ice, Franklin's crew abandoned their two ships, the *Erebus* and *Terror*, somewhere off the coast of King William Island and were never seen again.

I manage to stop at this remote part of the Arctic Archipelago on board an eight-day tour, uniquely led by a local Inuit team. In true expedition style, there are no promised ports of call as conditions can change suddenly. Our first two days' passage is devoid of ice or high seas, but we hear that another cruise ship has run aground in shallow straits to the far west. 'Even with the ice receding, there's only been clear passage here for about five years,' says Dugald Wells, President of Cruise North, a former marine engineer who has been working in the Arctic since the mid-1980s. 'I came up here because it was fun – a real frontier. It still is, but you have to respect the fact that only 50 per cent of these waters are surveyed,' he says.

Adapted from *The Independent*, 19 September 2010

1 What is the most noticeable feature of summer in the Arctic mentioned in paragraph 1 (after the introductory bold text)? *[1]*

....

2 Give two possible reasons as to why the writer describes the sled dogs as 'scrappy'. *[2]*

• ....

....

• ....

....

3 a Which word in paragraph 3 tells you that the box found by archaeologists had been buried
   in the ground?   *[1]*

     ....

  b What information did the Porter brothers hope that it would contain?   *[1]*

     ....

     ....

4 By referring to paragraph 4, explain why Sir John Franklin's ships were unsuited to the Arctic voyage. *[1]*

     ....

     ....

     ....

     ....

5 From paragraph 4, give two reasons why the British Admiralty placed so much importance on
   discovering the North-west Passage.   *[2]*

     • ....

     ....

     • ....

     ....

6 By referring to paragraph 5, explain fully, using your own words:

  a the writer's criticisms of Franklin's expedition   *[1]*

     ....

     ....

     ....

     ....

b the outcome of the expedition. *[1]*

....

....

7 Explain, using your own words, why the writer says in the final paragraph that on the Arctic tour, 'there are no promised ports of call'. *[1]*

....

....

....

....

Exercise 2

Read the following article carefully and then answer the questions which follow.

Experience: I was swept away by a flood

Vanessa Glover

'Shocked, tossed and buffeted, I gasped for breath and tried to keep my head above water.'

It was after midnight last December and we were driving home from a party. There had been extremely heavy rain on our journey there, though not enough to make us worry about the drive back. We were in our pick-up truck, which always felt safe. Paul, my husband, was driving and my seven-year-old son, Silas, was in the back.

What was so frightening was the speed of it. One minute we were halfway home and driving up to a familiar bridge, the next there was water rising over the bonnet. Deep floodwater was coursing across from a nearby railway line and surrounding fields, and we were caught in the middle of it.

The volume of water lifted our car up and pushed it back against a hedge. We were silent; I felt over-awed by the power of the water, and Paul was trying to control the truck.

Water was instantly around my ankles. I reached my hand back and felt it around Silas's, too. Paul climbed out through a window, at which point Silas woke up, confused and disoriented. I managed to pass him through the window to Paul, who was now on the truck's roof.

→

➔

Paul told me I needed to get out, but I couldn't open my door or window. I managed to push my body though the driver's window and was left clinging onto the support between the windows. I was terrified the truck would capsize, pinning me beneath. Paul was incredulous, asking me what I was doing in the water, and telling me I needed to climb onto the bonnet, but I couldn't reach.

He grabbed my hood to help, but I could hear Silas crying, so I told him to let go – Silas needed him. He refused, but I insisted – I wanted to know Silas would be OK. As I saw his empty, outstretched hand, the water took me away. I'm a strong swimmer, but had no option but to shoot down the rapids. Shocked, tossed and buffeted, I gasped for breath and tried to keep my head above water. There was a horrendously loud noise, like a huge wall of bubbles swirling in my ears. I never expected to die of drowning.

I was washed over a garden wall into the river, 3.5 m higher than normal and flowing at about 23 kph. It was extremely dark but I could just make out trees. I reached out and grabbed two branches no bigger than my index finger, with a perfect tight grip. Somehow my feet wedged in a firm foothold and I hugged the tree with my knees. Another minute, and I'd have been sucked beneath a railway bridge.

My plan was just to hold on. My body went into shock a few times and I trembled involuntarily. I told myself it was a natural response and concentrated on not losing my foothold. Not knowing if Paul and Silas were dead or alive, I thought that if they survived they would need me.

After nearly 40 minutes, I saw a small spotlight. I shouted for help. Someone glimpsed my movement and a firefighter tried to talk to me, but I couldn't hear her above the roar of the water.

The light of a helicopter made me out in the tree. Their heat-seeking equipment had traced me, but they could see I had no warmth in my lower body and were concerned I would become hypothermic and lose my grip. My husband, who had been rescued with my son in the bucket of a mechanical digger, was nearby with a policewoman. She reassured him that so long as they could hear me, there was hope.

Guided to me by the helicopter, the rescue team managed to steer the boat to my shoulder. Four strong arms lifted me into the boat and I felt sheer relief and utter safety.

My rescuers were volunteers who have since received medals and I have an incredibly deep bond with them. In the isolation of that tree, I found a strength of character I didn't know I possessed – but I'm still flabbergasted I survived at all.

Adapted from *The Guardian*, 15 June 2013

1 Why had the writer and her family been out late at night (paragraph 1, after the introductory bold text)? [1]

....

2 By referring closely to paragraphs 2 and 3, explain carefully what you learn about the flood and how it affected the car in which the writer was travelling. [3]

....

....

....

3 Using your own words, explain carefully Silas's state of mind when he woke up (paragraph 4). [2]

....

➔

....

4 Why was the writer afraid of the truck capsizing (paragraph 5)? [1]

....

5 What two things was the writer concerned about while she was hugging the tree (paragraph 8)? [2]

• ....

• ....

6 How can you tell how many people hauled the writer into the rescue boat (paragraph 11)? [1]

....

7 Which word in the final paragraph tells you that the writer was completely amazed by the outcome of her experience? [1]

....

Exercise 3

The following passage is an extract from the short story 'The Country of the Blind' by H.G. Wells. Nunez, an explorer in the Andes mountain range in South America, has fallen down a mountainside onto a rocky ledge where he has spent the night. Read the passage carefully and then answer the questions which follow.

He was awakened by the singing of birds in the trees far below.

He sat up and perceived he was at the foot of a vast precipice. Over against him another wall of rock reared itself against the sky. The gorge between these precipices ran east and west. It was full of the morning sunlight, which lit the mass of fallen mountain to the west. Below him it seemed there was a precipice equally steep, but behind the snow in the gully he found a sort of chimney-cleft dripping with snow-water, down which a desperate man might venture. He found it easier than it seemed and after a rock climb of no particular difficulty came to a steep slope of trees.

He turned his face up the gorge and saw it opened out above onto green meadows, among which he glimpsed a cluster of stone huts of unfamiliar fashion. At times his progress was like clambering along the face of a wall, and after a time the rising sun ceased to strike along the gorge, the voices of the singing birds died away, and the air grew cold and dark about him. But the distant valley with its houses was all the brighter for that. Among the rocks he noted an unfamiliar fern. He picked a frond or so and gnawed its stalk, and found it helpful.

About midday he came at last out of the gorge into the plain and the sunlight. He was stiff and weary; he sat down in the shadow of a rock, filled up his flask with water from a spring and drank it down. He remained for a time, resting before he went on to the houses.

They were very strange to his eyes, and indeed the whole appearance of that valley became, as he regarded it, stranger and more unfamiliar. The greater part of its surface was lush green meadow, starred with many beautiful flowers. It was irrigated with extraordinary care, and showed signs of systematic farming. High up and ringing the valley about was a wall, and what appeared to be a water channel, from which the little trickles of water that fed the meadow plants came. On the higher slopes flocks of llamas cropped the scanty grass. The irrigation streams ran together into a main channel down the centre of the valley, and this was enclosed on either side by a wall chest high. A number of paths paved with black and white stones, and each with a curious little kerb at the side, ran here and there in an orderly manner.

→

> The houses of the central village were quite unlike those of the mountain villages he knew. They stood in a continuous row on either side of a central street of astonishing cleanness. Here and there their walls were pierced by a door, but not a solitary window broke their even frontage. They were parti-coloured with extraordinary irregularity, smeared with a sort of plaster that was sometimes grey, sometimes drab, sometimes slate-coloured or dark brown. It was the sight of this wild plastering that made the explorer say to himself, 'The good man who did that must have been as blind as a bat.'
>
> He descended a steep place, and so came to the wall and channel that ran about the valley. He could now see a number of men and women resting on piled heaps of grass, as if taking a siesta, in the remoter part of the meadow. Nearer the village a number of children were lying on their backs, and then coming closer to him he saw three men. These men wore garments of llama cloth and boots and belts of leather, and caps of cloth with back and ear flaps. They followed one another in single file, walking slowly and yawning as they walked, like men who have been up all night. There was something so reassuringly prosperous and respectable in their bearing that after a moment's hesitation Nunez stood forward as conspicuously as possible upon his rock, and gave vent to a mighty shout that echoed round the valley.
>
> From 'The Country of the Blind' by H.G. Wells

1 What caused Nunez to wake up?   *[1]*

....

2 Using your own words, explain carefully how Nunez reached the slope of trees from the precipice
on which he awoke.   *[2]*

....

....

3 By referring closely to the second half of paragraph 2 ('He turned his face up the gorge ... and found
it helpful.'), state three things that the writer says that Nunez saw.   *[3]*

- ....

- ....

- ....

4 Why did the air grow 'cold and dark' (paragraph 2)?   *[1]*

....

....

....

5 Explain, using your own words, the sentence: 'It was irrigated with extraordinary care, and showed signs of systematic farming.' (paragraph 4). *[2]*

....

....

....

6 State two unusual things about the appearance of the village (paragraph 5). *[2]*

- ....

....

- ....

....

Writer's effects questions

As well as showing an understanding of the vocabulary used by writers another key skill that you need to develop is to understand (or appreciate) the way that writers use language to produce a particular response from their readers. The following group of questions allow you to practise both explaining the **meaning** of some key words in the passages on which they are based and also test your appreciation of how the writer's use of language creates a particular effect in the mind of the reader.

It is important to keep in mind that questions 3 and 4 in the following exercises ask you to explain *how* the language used by writers achieves particular effects. They do not ask you simply to explain the meanings of the words used. (Although it goes without saying that the best responses are likely to come from students who have a clear understanding of the meanings.)

In this section of the workbook, you will have the opportunity to practise writing answers to these types of questions in response to a range of passages.

The instructions for Exercise 4, question 4, on page 18 state that in order to answer the question, you should select 'powerful words and phrases' from the stimulus passage. It is also stated that the words or phrases chosen should contain **imagery**.

What is meant by imagery (and how to write about it)

Imagery means the use of figurative language (such as **simile**, **metaphor**, **onomatopoeia**, **alliteration**, **personification**, and so on) to represent objects, actions and ideas in such a way that there is an appeal to our physical senses. Imagery works initially by producing a picture in the mind of a reader. However, the range of associations with the vocabulary used by a writer to create the image is likely to produce secondary responses in the reader by appealing to other senses in addition to sight.

The basic tool that all writers use to communicate with their readers is their vocabulary – the words that they choose. For readers to understand what a writer is saying to them, it is important that they interpret the words as having the same meaning that the writers had in their minds when they chose them. This is particularly important in writing that is intended to give information or instruction. For example, if the reader of a medical textbook misunderstands the word *diseased* and assumes that the writer has written *deceased*, there may be considerable problems in store for future patients!

It is, of course, highly important that the vocabulary used in instructional writing should convey a clear and unambiguous meaning. However, in imaginative or personal writing, writers use language not to give instructions but in order to appeal to their readers' emotions and imaginations and to create a multi-dimensional response. One way by which this effect is achieved is when the reader responds not just to the meanings of the words in their immediate context, but to other associations that are carried by those words.

To take a straightforward example – if you hear someone shout the word *duck*, what does that mean to you? If you are an ornithologist, your first thought will be of a feathered flying creature. If you are in a school playground, you might respond by lowering your head or throwing yourself on the ground to avoid a flying missile. If you are a cricketer, you are likely to assume that the batsman has not been very successful. Or, if your mind is not focused on anything in particular, you might respond by associating any or all of these meanings together!

Such a reaction as that mentioned above is not highly likely when the different meanings of a word (such as *duck*) are clearly distinct. However, in much imaginative writing, the associations of the words used by a writer are much more closely linked. Readers who are fully engaged in the text will respond to what the writer has written by adding their own responses to the vocabulary and thereby creating a more complex response to what they are reading. This is sometimes referred to as responding to meanings *beyond the literal*.

Some figures of speech

The intention of the previous paragraphs was to help you to understand what you should do when you are asked to comment on a writer's use of language in the phrases you have chosen. Although it is important to show a clear understanding of the writer's overall intention, you must also do your best to show how your interpretation of the vocabulary, and the imagery that it creates, helps to develop and communicate the full implications of the writer's intention.

Writers create imagery through the use of figures of speech. There is not space here to provide an exhaustive list of the different figures of speech that can be found, nor is it appropriate to do so. However, below is a brief list of the main figures of speech that are likely to occur in the passages that you will read, together with definitions and examples of their use.

Simile

A simile is a direct comparison between two things, introduced by the word *like* or *as*, in order to make a description more vivid or emphatic. For example, in John Steinbeck's novel *Of Mice and Men*, the following phrase is used to describe the relationship between the mentally challenged character Lennie and his friend and protector George.

> ## Key point
>
> When commenting on a writer's use of language, it is important to keep in mind that you should comment on *how* writers achieve their effects and not *what* figures of speech they use in order to do so. It is not enough simply to identify similes, metaphors, etc. in a piece of writing – it is necessary to explain what the *effects* of their use are on a reader.

Lennie is like a terrier who doesn't want to bring its ball to its master.

The comparison between Lennie and a dog helps to convey to the reader that Lennie's intelligence is little more than that of an animal. It also presents a more sympathetic picture of him by showing that he is both dependent on his friend as well as being a little afraid that he may have done something to upset him for which he may be scolded.

Metaphor

A metaphor is an indirect comparison in which one thing is expressed in terms of another – there is no need to use *like* or *as*. For example, a character in one of Shakespeare's plays says that:

All the world's a stage and all the men and women merely players.

He is not suggesting that literally everyone in the world lives and performs inside a theatre, but is using the comparison between the world and a stage in a symbolic way to suggest that we all behave ('act') in different ways in different circumstances.

Onomatopoeia

Onomatopoeia is a term used to describe the effect created by a writer when the sound of a word or words echoes the sense of what is being described, and helps to bring the description alive in the mind of the reader. In its simplest form, words like *bang* and *crash* are examples of onomatopoeia. A more complex example is the following description from W.B. Yeats's poem *The Lake Isle of Innisfree*:

Nine bean-rows will I have there, a hive for the honey-bee;

And live alone in the bee-loud glade.

The description of the peace of the island is enhanced for the reader as the vowel sounds in 'alone in the bee-loud glade' echo the humming of the bees that the poet is describing.

Alliteration

Alliteration is the term given to the repetition of the same sound(s) at the beginning of words. At its simplest level, this is the main device used in tongue-twisters such as 'Peter Piper picked a peck of pickled pepper'. However, in D.H. Lawrence's poem *Snake*, the repetition of the 's' sound at the start of the words in the following lines very effectively suggests the hissing sound of a snake:

He sipped with his straight mouth,

Softly drank through his straight gums, into his slack long body,

Silently.

Personification

Personification is the term given to the literary technique of attributing human characteristics to inanimate objects or non-human life forms, as in the following famous lines from William Wordsworth's description of a wood full of daffodils:

Ten thousand saw I at a glance,

Tossing their heads in sprightly dance.

The description of the flowers, which suggests that they were like exuberant and carefree human dancers, gives a vivid impression of the scene and also helps the readers to identify with the poet's response to the flowers.

> ## Key point
>
> The use of one figure of speech can easily blend in with that of another. In the example of alliteration from the poem *Snake*, the lines also have an onomatopoeic effect, and the example of personification is also a type of metaphor. As mentioned earlier, you should not worry too much about identifying examples of figures of speech – what is important is that you recognise their *effect* on a reader and then explain *how* this effect is achieved.

Although the use of literary devices such as those mentioned above is the main way in which writers create imagery, you might also need to consider how things such as sentence structure and the length of sentences contribute to the overall effect that a writer achieves.

The different types of questions in the following exercises test both your understanding of the vocabulary used in the accompanying passages and of how the writer of the passage has used language to create particular responses in a reader's mind.

- Question 1 requires you to write down words or phrases from the text with the same meaning as those underlined in four sentences given in the question. Note that when answering this question it is important that you write down only the word or group of words that relate directly to those that you are defining.

- Question 2 requires you to explain in your own words the meanings of three words used in the passage. Note that it is important when answering this question that you explain only the words underlined in the question, that you explain the word in the context of the passage in which it occurs and that you do not use the same word as a different part of speech in your answer – for example, it would be wrong to define the word 'scream' in the following sentence 'The child gave a scream of excitement on opening his present' by saying 'screamed excitedly'. If you cannot think of a single word to replace that underlined in the question, it is permissible to use a short phrase to define it.

- Question 3 requires you to explain in your own words how specific words or phrases used by the writer in a short section of the passage suggest particular atmosphere, experience or feelings. Note that when responding to this question it is important that you give evidence that you have some appreciation of the appropriate associations and suggestions in the writer's choice of words.

- Question 4 refers you to two sections of the passage and then requires you to select four words or phrases from each section (that is, eight words or phrases in total) that produce a particular effect or response in the mind of the reader. You should explain how each of your selections is used effectively in the context of the passage. Note that in answering this question, it is important that you show understanding and appreciation of the imagery used by the writer and that you focus on explaining *how* the language creates a particular effect and not on simply identifying and naming any figures of speech that you recognise.

Example of a writer's effects questions

The following passage is a satirical description of a lesson in a school in 19th-century England, taken from the opening of Charles Dickens's *Hard Times*. Answer the questions which follow.

'Now, what I want is, Facts. Teach these boys and girls nothing but Facts. Facts alone are wanted in life. Plant nothing else, and root out everything else. You can only form the minds of reasoning animals upon Facts: nothing else will ever be of any service to them. This is the principle on which I bring up my own children, and this is the principle on which I bring up these children. Stick to Facts, sir!'

The scene was **a plain, bare, monotonous vault of a school-room** (1), and the speaker's square forefinger emphasised his observations by underscoring every sentence with a line on the schoolmaster's sleeve. The emphasis was helped by **the speaker's square wall of a forehead, which had his eyebrows for its base** (2), while his eyes found commodious cellarage in two dark caves, overshadowed by the wall. The emphasis was helped by the speaker's mouth, which was wide, thin, and hard set. The emphasis was helped by the speaker's voice, which was inflexible, dry, and dictatorial. The emphasis was helped by **the speaker's hair, which bristled on the skirts of his bald head, a plantation of firs to keep the wind from its shining surface** (3), all covered with knobs, like the crust of a plum pie, **as if the head had scarcely warehouse-room for the hard facts stored inside** (4). The speaker's obstinate carriage, square coat, square legs, square shoulders,—nay, his very neckcloth, trained to take him by the throat with an unaccommodating grasp, like a stubborn fact, as it was,—all helped the emphasis.

'In this life, we want nothing but Facts, sir; nothing but Facts!'

The speaker, and the schoolmaster, and the third grown person present, all backed a little, and swept with their eyes the inclined plane of little vessels then and there arranged in order, ready to have imperial gallons of facts poured into them until they were full to the brim.

From *Hard Times* by Charles Dickens

1 Identify a word or phrase from the text which conveys the same idea as the words underlined:

a He thought that facts were essential for shaping the minds of <u>rational beings</u>.

(Answer: reasoning animals)

b It is on this <u>premise</u> that I have based the education of my children.

(Answer: principle)

c The underground cavern provided <u>large storage space</u> for his equipment.

(Answer: commodious cellarage)

d He spoke to us in such a <u>domineering</u> way that we had to do what he said.

(Answer: dictatorial)

2 Explain, in your own words, what the writer means by each of the words underlined:

'The speaker's <u>obstinate</u> carriage, square coat, square legs, square shoulders,—nay, his very neckcloth, trained to take him by the throat with an <u>unaccommodating</u> grasp, like a stubborn fact, as it was,—all helped the <u>emphasis</u>.'

a obstinate

(Answer: inflexible / refusal to change his mind)

b unaccommodating

(Answer: uncooperative / intractable / not accepting other suggestions)

c emphasis

(Answer: forcefulness / weight / stress)

3 Explain, in your own words, how the underlined phrases are used by the writer to suggest the character of the speaker:

'The speaker's <u>obstinate carriage</u>, square coat, square legs, square shoulders,—nay, his very neckcloth, trained to <u>take him by the throat with an unaccommodating grasp,</u> like a stubborn fact, as it was,—<u>all helped the emphasis</u>.'

(Answer: The words 'obstinate carriage' suggest that the speaker is like a heavy and inflexible vehicle that once moving cannot be stopped. 'Take him by the throat with an unaccommodating grasp' further suggests that the speaker is rough and violent in defence of his beliefs and will use force to ensure that others agree with him. 'All helped the emphasis' implies that the speaker will use all of his strength and threatening nature to force home his ideas on other people in the room.)

4   Re-read the second paragraph of the passage and then select four powerful words and phrases that suggest the appearance of the school-room and the appearance and attitude of the man speaking. Your choices should include imagery. Explain how each of your chosen words or phrases is used in the context of the passage.

(Answer: See below)

Student response

1   a plain, bare, monotonous vault of a school-room

The vocabulary in this phrase is direct and unadorned, reflecting the plain, uninteresting nature of the room. The list of three adjectives ('plain, bare, monotonous') builds up to emphasise effectively the stultifying surroundings in which the lesson is taking place. The noun 'vault' carries associations not just of a vast, empty space, but also hints that the room is like a cold burial chamber, reinforcing the idea that the school-room is part of the means by which the life of imagination is denied, as conveyed by the final line of the passage.

2   the speaker's square wall of a forehead, which had his eyebrows for its base

As befits someone who is in favour of only 'facts' being taught, the forehead of the speaker is described as 'square', which suggests that there is no scope for deviation from straight lines in his way of thinking. 'Wall' suggests solidity and the main purpose of a wall is to keep out trespassers; in this case, imaginative ideas. The image of the man as a mathematical creation is reinforced by the description of his eyebrows as being the base of the wall – 'base' is a word associated with triangles as well as walls.

3   the speaker's hair, which bristled on the skirts of his bald head, a plantation of firs to keep the wind from its shining surface

This is a mainly comic image which encourages the reader to see the man as someone deserving to be laughed at. (The writer is, after all, satirising his attitude and ideas.) The description of his hair as 'bristling' suggests that there is something about him that is looking to take offence. The metaphorical phrase ('a plantation of firs') again reinforces the point that his purpose is to prevent any unwanted thoughts (as suggested by the wind) from entering his mind.

4   as if the head had scarcely warehouse-room for the hard facts stored inside

Following on from the image of the 'vault' earlier in the passage, the word 'warehouse-room' conveys the idea of the speaker's mind, like the classroom, being a place in which commodities are stored. The commodities in this case are 'hard facts' – again, there is no need for any imagination in the speaker's outlook. The description of the facts as 'hard' suggests that they are harsh and unfriendly.

Practice exercises

Now is your opportunity to put into practice what you have learnt about commenting on the way writers use language. The following six passages are all examples of descriptive writing, but are in a range of styles and written for a variety of purposes. They are all followed by exercises that provide a focus for your comments and are all suitable practice for Question 2 on Paper 1. Some phrases have been highlighted in each passage to give an indication of suitable descriptions to comment on. However, as these exercises are intended to provide you with practice for answering this type of question in an examination, you should feel free to choose other phrases from the passages if you wish.

Exercise 4

The following passage is taken from the comic novel *The Third Policeman* by the Irish writer Flann O'Brien. In this extract, the narrator breaks into what he thinks is an empty house to look for a metal box hidden beneath the floorboards. Answer the questions which follow.

The Third Policeman

I opened the iron gate and walked as softly as I could up the weed-tufted gravel drive. My mind was strangely empty. I felt no glow of pleasure and was unexcited at the prospect of becoming rich. I was occupied only with the mechanical task of finding a black box.

The front-door was closed and set far back in a very deep porch. **The wind and rain had whipped a coating of gritty dust against the panels** and deep into the crack where the door opened, showing that it had been shut for years. Standing on a derelict flower-bed, I tried to push open the first window on the left. **It yielded to my strength, raspingly and stubbornly.** I clambered through the opening and found myself, not at once in a room, but crawling along the deepest window-ledge I had ever seen. After I had jumped noisily down upon the floor, I looked up and the open window seemed very far away and much too small to have admitted me.

The room where I found myself was thick with dust, musty and empty of all furniture. Spiders had erected great stretchings of their web about the fireplace. I made my way quickly to the hall, threw open the door of the room where the box was and paused on the threshold. It was a dark morning and **the weather had stained the windows with blears of grey wash** which kept the brightest part of the weak light from coming in. The far corner of the room was a blur of shadow. **I had a sudden urge to have done with my task and be out of this house forever.** I walked across the bare boards, knelt down in the corner and passed my hands about the floor in search of the loose board. To my surprise I found it easily. It was about two feet in length and rocked hollowly under my hand. I lifted it up, laid it aside and struck a match. I saw a black metal cash-box nestling dimly in the hole. I put my hand down and crooked a finger into the loose reclining handle but the match suddenly flickered and went out and the handle of the box, which I had lifted up about an inch, slid heavily off my finger. Without stopping to light another match, I thrust my hand into the opening and, just when it should be closing about the box, something happened.

I cannot hope to describe what it was but it had frightened me very much. It was some change which came upon me or upon the room, indescribably subtle, yet momentous. **It was as if the daylight had changed with unnatural suddenness,** as if the temperature had altered greatly in an instant or as if the air had become twice as rare or twice as dense as it had been in the twinkling of an eye. Perhaps all of these, or other things, happened together, for all my senses were bewildered all at once and could give me no explanation. The fingers of my right hand, thrust in the opening in the floor, had closed mechanically, found nothing at all, and came up again empty. The box had gone!

I heard a cough behind me, soft and natural, yet more disturbing than any sound that could ever come upon the human ear. That I did not die of fright was due, I think, to two things: the fact that **my senses were already disarranged** and able to interpret to me only gradually what they had perceived and also the fact that the utterance of the cough seemed to bring with it some more awful alteration in everything. **It was as if the universe stood still for an instant, suspending the planets in their courses.** I collapsed weakly from my kneeling, backwards into a limp sitting-down position upon the floor. Sweat broke out on my brow and my eyes remained open for a long time without a wink, glazed and almost sightless.

In the darkest corner of the room, near the window, a man was sitting in a chair, eyeing me with a mild but unwavering interest.

From *The Third Policeman* by Flann O'Brien

Photocopying prohibited

1 Identify a word or phrase from the text which conveys the same idea as the underlined words:

a He thought the <u>possibility of finding a fortune</u> was highly unlikely.

....

b It <u>gave way</u> as I pushed it.

....

c He <u>stopped briefly before entering the room</u> and listened carefully.

....

d He felt an <u>abrupt impulse</u> to run away as quickly as possible.

....

2 Explain, in your own words, what the writer means by each of the underlined words:

'Perhaps all of these, or other things, happened together, for all my senses were <u>bewildered</u> all at once and could give me no explanation. The fingers of my right hand, <u>thrust</u> in the opening in the floor, had closed <u>mechanically</u>, found nothing at all, and came up again empty.'

....

....

3 Explain, in your own words, how the underlined phrases are used by the writer to suggest the character of the speaker:

'Perhaps all of these, or other things, happened together, for all my <u>senses were bewildered all at once</u> and could give me no explanation. The fingers of my right hand, <u>thrust in the opening in the floor</u>, had <u>closed mechanically, found nothing at all</u>, and came up again empty.'

....

4 Re-read the passage and then select four powerful words and phrases that suggest the atmosphere both in and outside the house and the thoughts and feelings of the narrator. Your choices should include imagery. Explain how each of your chosen words or phrases is used in the context of the passage.

....

....

....

....

....

....

....

....

....

....

....

Exercise 5

This is a newspaper article in which the writer describes her frightening experience of being caught up in an earthquake while staying at her holiday home in a village near Rome. Answer the questions which follow.

I was in an earthquake

Amanda Austen

Half asleep, I couldn't work out what was happening. I hesitated in waking up Nick, my husband, because I thought I was probably being too dramatic. ***Then the tremors moved up a gear*** and the whole house began to shake – ***it sounded like an old train carriage rattling, shifting backwards and forwards***, then side to side. It was a bone-jarring feeling. Help, I thought, this is an earthquake. I shook Nick awake – if I was going to die, I didn't want to be alone. He had been fast asleep and woke up with a shock.

Looking back now, I wonder why we didn't run out of the house, as far away as possible. Yet our instinct was to stay put. So we clung to each other in bed, terrified and waiting for the worst to happen. ***The earth rumbling below us was such a disorienting feeling***; all I could imagine was a crack opening up beneath me and then me falling in.

We watched as household objects slid and then crashed to the floor, wondering where it would end. And then it stopped, just like that. The whole experience had lasted less than a minute. ***All that noise and movement was replaced by eerie silence.*** Everything was still except for a gaudy gold chandelier that we had inherited and that now swung from side to side.

Adapted from *The Guardian*, 30 May 2009

1   Identify a word or phrase from the text which conveys the same idea as the underlined words:

   a   I paused for a moment and thought about telling my husband.

   ....

   b   If I woke him, he might think I was being too excitable.

   ....

   c   Our initial inclination was to wait and see what happened.

   ....

   d   Some of the fittings in the room were rather flashy and ostentatious.

   ....

2   Explain, in your own words, what the writer means by each of the underlined words:

   'The whole experience had lasted less than a minute. All that noise and movement was replaced by eerie silence. Everything was still except for a gaudy gold chandelier that we had inherited and that now swung from side to side.'

   ....

   ....

   ....

3   Explain, in your own words, how the following phrases are used by the writer to suggest the after effects of the earthquake:

   a   'The whole experience had lasted less than a minute.'

   ....

   ....

   b   'All that noise and movement was replaced by eerie silence.'

   ....

   ....

   c   'Everything was still except for a gaudy gold chandelier that we had inherited and that now swung from side to side.'

   ....

4 Re-read the passage and then select eight powerful words and phrases that suggest the experience of being in an earthquake and the thoughts and feelings of the narrator. Your choices should include imagery. Explain how each of your chosen words or phrases is used in the context of the passage.

- ....
- ....
- ....
- ....
- ....
- ....
- ....
- ....

Exercise 6

This is an extract from the novel *The Lost World* by Sir Arthur Conan Doyle. It describes the experiences of a group of adventurers in an unexplored part of South America. Answer the questions which follow.

It was indeed a wonderful place. Having reached the spot marked by a line of light-green rushes, we poled our two canoes through them for some hundreds of yards, and eventually emerged into a placid and shallow stream, running clear and transparent over a sandy bottom. It may have been twenty yards across, and was banked in on each side by most luxuriant vegetation. No one who had not observed that for a short distance reeds had taken the place of shrubs, could possibly have guessed the existence of such a stream or dreamed of the fairyland beyond.

For a fairyland it was—the most wonderful that the imagination of man could conceive. The thick vegetation met overhead, interlacing into a natural pergola, and through this tunnel of verdure in a golden twilight flowed the green, pellucid river, beautiful in itself, *but marvellous from the strange tints thrown by the vivid light from above filtered and tempered in its fall*. Clear as crystal, motionless as a sheet of glass, green as the edge of an iceberg, it stretched in front of us under its leafy archway, every stroke of our paddles sending a thousand ripples across its shining surface. It was a fitting avenue to a land of wonders. All sign of human life had passed away, but animal life was more frequent, and the tameness of the creatures showed that they knew nothing of the hunter. Fuzzy little black-velvet monkeys, with snow-white teeth and gleaming, mocking eyes, chattered at us as we passed. With a dull, heavy splash an occasional cayman plunged in from the bank. *Once a dark, clumsy tapir stared at us from a gap in the bushes, and then lumbered away through the forest*; once, too, the yellow, sinuous form of a great puma whisked amid the brushwood, and *its green, baleful eyes glared hatred at us over its tawny shoulder*. Bird life was abundant, especially the wading birds, stork, heron, and ibis gathering in little groups, blue, scarlet, and white, upon every log which jutted from the bank, while beneath us the crystal water was alive with fish of every shape and colour.

For three days we made our way up this tunnel of hazy green sunshine. On the longer stretches one could hardly tell as one looked ahead where the distant green water ended and the distant green archway began. The deep peace of this strange waterway was unbroken by any sign of man.

From *The Lost World* by Sir Arthur Conan Doyle

1 Identify a word or phrase from the text which conveys the same idea as the underlined words:

a At this point the river was <u>peaceful and not very deep.</u>

....

b In the forest we were surrounded by extremely <u>lush foliage.</u>

....

c We paddled our canoes through a channel <u>closed in by greenery.</u>

....

d The monkeys with their <u>bright eyes were making fun of us.</u>

....

2 Explain, in your own words, what the writer means by each of the underlined words:

'For three days we made our way up this tunnel of <u>hazy</u> green sunshine. On the longer <u>stretches</u> one could hardly tell as one looked ahead where the distant green water ended and the distant green archway began. The deep peace of this strange waterway was <u>unbroken</u> by any sign of man.'

....

....

3 Explain, in your own words, how the underlined phrases are used by the writer to suggest the atmosphere and appearance of the surroundings of their journey:

'For three days <u>we made our way up this tunnel of hazy green sunshine. On the longer stretches one could hardly tell as one looked ahead where the distant green water ended and the distant green archway began. The deep peace of this strange waterway was unbroken by any sign of man.</u>'

....

....

....

....

4 Re-read the passage and then select eight powerful words and phrases that convey the narrator's impressions of both the scenery and the animal and bird life that he experiences. Your choices should include imagery. Explain how each of your chosen words or phrases is used in the context of the passage.

• ....

• ....

- ....
- ....
- ....
- ....
- ....
- ....

Exercise 7

This passage is an extract from a short story entitled 'The Scream', which describes the feelings of a young girl, Anna, during a ride on a roller-coaster. Answer the questions which follow.

The front car gave a lurch forwards, and the five other cars followed jerkily. Anna was strapped helplessly to the seat, and paralysed by fear, unable to twist her head or do anything except seal her eyes shut against the red lights fading behind her as the roller-coaster advanced into the tunnel.

At first it was like being on a train. The rocking motion of the car over the uneven track, and the rhythmic pounding against the underside of the car. *She felt like a baby being rocked to sleep with the approach of night and the enveloping blackness of the tunnel.* Feeling the sudden warmth of the sun on her chilled limbs, Anna became aware that they had emerged into the daylight, and were now slowly ascending a steep section of the course. The car was tipped at such an angle, Anna lay almost horizontally against the back of her seat. She prayed for the climb to go on and on, never reaching its peak so that she would not have to suffer the speedy descent. She was rigid with terror at the very thought of it.

Anna felt the car teetering on the brink at the high point of the track, sure they would either tumble backwards or forwards, she snapped open her eyes for a split second, long enough to see the two silver runners of the track sliding down the other side of the mountain, *before her breath was torn from her lungs along with the forming scream which fizzled to nothing, as they plunged head first towards the ground*.

It was not a straight drop. There was a violent bend in the track half way down and Anna was thrown sideways against the protective metal bar as the car swung round into a corkscrew spin, winding down, down, only to level out literally metres above the concrete.

Anna gulped in air and the car began to rise again, a ceiling of azure sky visible behind the black frame. She could hear the creak of the cable pulling the car against the gravity, straining with the tension. Please don't let it break, her mind called out. Plummeting down the other side, she became conscious of the deafening shrieks and cries from the cars behind her. *One person screamed and the others copied, one by one like falling dominoes, cries of mock horror and pretend fear.* Anna's fear was real, embedded deep inside her like an icicle in her heart. She was suffocating, incapable of taking in oxygen with the scream wedged in her throat. The roller-coaster pulled out of its dive and into the first loop, Anna hanging disorientated the wrong way up, her legs jammed into the metal bar, the blood rushing to her head. There was hardly time to catch her breath before the roller-coaster launched into the second, moving faster and faster, the world spinning, dizzy. The third and final loop rushed by; Anna barely noticed – to her they seemed to all run into one horrific spiral.

The chain of golden cars were going up again for the last time, unhurried, creeping inch by inch. Hurry, pleaded Anna to herself, get it over with, let me die soon. She was filled with apprehension, dreading the near vertical drop. *High in the air, Anna could see the entire expanse of the theme park spread out beneath, miniature people scurrying from place to place like hungry insects.* She saw the tiny camera half hidden at the top, and the faint flash as she sped past it, already on her way to the bottom. The wind flew past her ears, catching hold of her hair and making it stand out behind. Her stomach left her body, suspended in the air as she proceeded on without it. Her fear abandoned her and at last she could scream, as loudly as was possible, the rest of the way down.

From 'The Scream' by H. Briscoe

1   Identify a word or phrase from the text which conveys the same idea as the underlined words:

a   Kim's first driving lesson began as the car took off <u>with a jerk.</u>

....

b   His father in the passenger seat was <u>so frightened he could not move.</u>

....

c   With his heart <u>hammering</u> against his chest, Kim tried again.

....

d   His father felt the car <u>falling sharply out of control.</u>

....

2   Explain, in your own words, what the writer means by each of the underlined words:

'Anna's fear was real, <u>embedded</u> deep inside her like an icicle in her heart. She was suffocating, incapable of taking in oxygen with the scream <u>wedged</u> in her throat. The roller-coaster pulled out of its dive and into the first loop, Anna hanging <u>disorientated</u> the wrong way up, her legs jammed into the metal bar….'

....

....

3   Explain, in your own words, how the underlined phrases are used by the writer to suggest Anna's experience during the roller-coaster ride:

'Anna's fear was real, <u>embedded deep inside her like an icicle in her heart</u>. She was <u>suffocating, incapable of taking in oxygen with the scream wedged in her throat</u>. The roller-coaster pulled out of its dive and into the first loop, <u>Anna hanging disorientated the wrong way up, her legs jammed into the metal bar</u>….'

....

....

....

....

4   Re-read the passage and then select eight powerful words and phrases that convey Anna's thoughts and feelings during her roller-coaster ride experience. Your choices should include imagery. Explain how each of your chosen words or phrases is used in the context of the passage.

   •   ....

   •   ....

- ....

- ....

- ....

- ....

- ....

- ....

Exercise 8

This is a further extract from the article about the North-west Passage by Sarah Barrell that you came across earlier in this workbook. In the following paragraphs, the writer describes her experience of swimming in the cold Arctic waters and the wildlife that is found there. Answer the questions which follow.

During the day, when landings allow, those of us holding out for the big mammal show – polar bears, caribou and ***humorously hirsute musk ox*** – take hopeful walks along unmapped beaches, guarded by armed crew strategically stationed on higher ground. But on rocky hillsides we mostly unearth the smaller of the Arctic species: miniature meadows of shimmering cotton grass, tiny forests of Arctic willow. 'You're walking in the tree tops!' beams the ship's botanist, Liz Bradfield, as we trot unseeing past the heroic fauna that stands no more than 3 centimetres above the harsh tundra. It's easy to work up a heat walking in five layers of thermal clothing. Bit by bit, layers are peeled off until, one sunny day, a much-vaunted 'polar bear' swim is initiated. Those of the crew who don't go in stand by with essential Arctic beach kit: thick towels and a defibrillator.

The water is thick with chunks of ice that dwarf our sizeable Zodiac inflatable boats, and it's just a notch above freezing. I wade in and am out again in agonising seconds, although my feet take 10 minutes to stop throbbing. Daniel Scott, a more hardy soul, goes in with mask and snorkel. As does the ship's tireless marine biologist, Marie-Josee Desbarats, motivated not by the kudos of taking an Arctic plunge but to get a closer look at the near-microscopic creatures submerged in the ice floe.

Bearded seals flop on and off the steaming ice floe, a musk ox is seen grazing on the mossy hillside and, within minutes, finally, polar bears have been spotted. ***A mother and baby bear, agile as mountain goats, come down a steep rock face, settling on the beach to watch us bob around on the Zodiacs just offshore.*** For at least 15 minutes we observe one another, our group more open-mouthed than theirs, before they trot casually back up the cliff.

During the next few days we would all be staggered by such close encounters with wildlife. ***One afternoon we get within near-petting distance of two snoozy Arctic hares that sit at our feet like plump white pillows*** while we take endless photos. We move off before they do. Another morning before digesting our own breakfast, the Zodiacs get within 10 metres of a narwhal on the shores of Devon Island. He seems as unfazed by us as is ***the vast musk ox that crosses our path with the nonchalant swagger of a cowboy*** as we are trekking later that day. 'You can pretty much guarantee that for these animals, this is their first encounter with humans,' says expedition leader Jason Annahatak as we continue on our way around yet another aptly unnamed bay.

Adapted from *The Independent*, 19 September 2010

1 Identify a word or phrase from the text which conveys the same idea as the underlined words:

   a The guards were <u>positioned judiciously</u> to protect us without their being seen.

   ....

   b The snow-covered ground was <u>glistening brightly</u> in the sun.

   ....

   c The experience of swimming with polar bears was <u>highly recommended</u>.

   ....

   d The water temperature was only <u>marginally more</u> than I could stand.

   ....

2 Explain, in your own words, what the writer means by each of the underlined words:

   'I <u>wade in</u> and am out again in agonising seconds, although my feet take 10 minutes to stop <u>throbbing</u>. Daniel Scott, a more <u>hardy</u> soul, goes in with mask and snorkel. As does the ship's tireless marine biologist, Marie-Josee Desbarats...'

   ....

   ....

3 Explain, in your own words, how the underlined phrases are used by the writer to express the reactions of herself and her companions to the swim in Arctic waters:

   '<u>I wade in and am out again in agonising seconds</u>, although <u>my feet take 10 minutes to stop throbbing. Daniel Scott, a more hardy soul</u>, goes in with mask and snorkel. As does the ship's tireless marine biologist</u>, Marie-Josee Desbarats...'

   ....

   ....

   ....

   ....

4 Re-read the passage and then select eight powerful words and phrases that convey the writer's impressions and feelings about the living creatures that she came across during her time in the Arctic. Your choices should include imagery. Explain how each of your chosen words or phrases is used in the context of the passage.

   • ....

   • ....

- ....
- ....
- ....
- ....
- .... =
- ....

Exercise 9

This is an extract from *My Family and Other Animals* by the naturalist Gerald Durrell. In this passage he describes Achilles, a tortoise that he kept as a pet when he was a child and he and his family were living on the Greek island of Corfu. Answer the questions which follow.

The new arrival was christened Achilles, and turned out to be *a most intelligent and lovable beast, possessed of an unusual sense of humour*. At first he was tied up by a leg in the garden, but as he grew tamer we let him go where he pleased. He learnt his name in a very short time, and we had only to call out once or twice and then wait patiently for a while and he would appear, lumbering along the narrow stone paths on tip-toe, his head and neck stretched out eagerly. *He loved being fed, and would squat regally in the sun while we held out bits of lettuce, dandelions, or grapes for him.* He loved grapes as much as Roger our dog did, so there was always great rivalry. Achilles would sit mumbling the grapes in his mouth, the juice running down his chin, and Roger would lie nearby, watching him with agonised eyes, his mouth drooling saliva.

But the fruit that Achilles liked best were wild strawberries. He would become very excited at the mere sight of them, *lumbering to and fro, craning his head to see if you were going to give him any, gazing at you pleadingly with his tiny boot-button eyes*. The very small strawberries he could devour at a gulp, for they were only the size of a fat pea. But if you gave him a big one, say the size of a hazelnut, he behaved in a way unlike any other tortoise I have ever seen. He would grab the fruit and, holding it firmly in his mouth, would stumble off at top speed until he reached a safe and secluded spot among the flower-beds, where he would drop the fruit and then eat it at leisure, returning for another one when he had finished.

As well as developing a passion for strawberries, Achilles also developed a passion for human company. Let anyone come into the garden to sit and sun-bathe, to read or for any other reason and before long there would be a rustling among the grass, and Achilles's wrinkled face would be poked through. If you were sitting in a chair, he contented himself with getting as close to your feet as possible, and there he would sink into a deep and peaceful sleep, his head drooping out of his shell, his nose resting on the ground. *If, however, you were lying on a rug, sun-bathing, Achilles would be convinced that you were lying on the ground simply in order to provide him with amusement.*

He would surge down the path and onto the rug with an expression of bemused good humour on his face. He would pause, look at you thoughtfully, and then choose a portion of your anatomy on which to practise mountaineering. Suddenly to have the sharp claws of a determined tortoise embedded in your thigh as he tries to lever himself up onto your stomach is not conducive to relaxation. If you shook him off and moved the rug it would only give you temporary respite, for Achilles would circle the garden grimly until he found you again. This habit became so tiresome that, after many complaints and threats from the family, I had to lock him up whenever we lay in the garden.

From *My Family and Other Animals* by Gerald Durrell

1 Identify a word or phrase from the text which conveys the same idea as the underlined words:

   a Achilles was <u>trundling</u> through the garden in search of wild strawberries.

   ....

   b The tortoise was <u>dribbling profusely</u> as he ate the strawberries he was given.

   ....

   c He <u>bolted down</u> the small strawberries <u>in one mouthful</u>.

   ....

   d He was sometimes shy and took his food to <u>a tucked-away part</u> of the garden to eat it.

   ....

2 Explain, in your own words, what the writer means by each of the words underlined:

   'Suddenly to have the sharp claws of a <u>determined</u> tortoise embedded in your thigh as he tries to lever himself up onto your stomach is not <u>conducive</u> to relaxation. If you shook him off and moved the rug it would only give you temporary <u>respite</u>, for Achilles would circle the garden grimly until he found you again.'

   ....

   ....

3 Explain, in your own words, how the underlined phrases are used by the writer to suggest the feelings of the family and himself towards Achilles' attempts to be friendly:

   '<u>Suddenly to have the sharp claws of a determined tortoise embedded in your thigh</u> as he tries <u>to lever himself up onto your stomach is not conducive to relaxation</u>. If you shook him off and moved the rug <u>it would only give you temporary respite, for Achilles would circle the garden grimly until he found you</u> again.'

   ....

   ....

   ....

   ....

4 Re-read the passage and then select eight powerful words and phrases that convey the character and appearance of Achilles, the tortoise. Your choices should include imagery. Explain how each of your chosen words or phrases is used in the context of the passage.

   • ....

   • ....

- ....
- ....
- ....
- ....
- ....
- ....

2 Directed writing

Other ways of testing your reading skills are questions which ask you to write at length in response to a passage that you have read. Some questions will ask for an extended response to reading and expect you to build on your understanding of the passage that you have read through producing a descriptive or narrative piece of writing. On the other hand, Directed Writing questions will require a discursive or argumentative treatment of key points from the source passage and involve a more critical, evaluative consideration of its content. Remember that these questions test both your reading and writing skills.

It is important that you spend a considerable part of your time on reading to ensure that you have understood the passage as fully as you can. You should try to keep your answers to about 200–250 words – if you try to write too much, it is extremely likely that your answer will be unfocused and contain errors of expression caused by carelessness and haste.

Key points

All directed writing tasks will give you an audience and a context for your writing. It is important that, as far as possible, you use a register in your writing that is suitable for the audience.

If you write in a style similar to that of the original passage you will have shown that you have appreciated the language of the writer and you should be credited for this.

Extended response to reading exercises

The practice exercises on the following pages provide you with tasks to practise your skills in building on the content and ideas of a reading passage. (Some of the passages are the same as those in Section 1 to provide practice in answering short-answer comprehension questions. You might like to start by answering these as the work you have already done in answering the comprehension questions should help you in writing your answers.)

Note

In the following exercises, there are two or three questions set on each passage to provide you with practice for this type of question. However, remember that in the examination only *one* directed writing question will be set on the reading passage.

For each practice question, you should base your response on what you have read in the passage but you should not copy from it. You should attempt to use your own words throughout. Your answer should address and develop all three points in the question.

Exercise 1

Read carefully the following extract from the article about the North-west Passage by Sarah Barrell. Then answer the questions which follow.

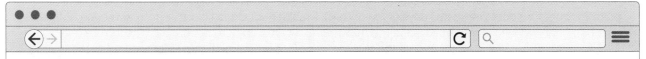

The North-west Passage: A 21st-century expedition

Sarah Barrell

A cruise, led by Inuit people, follows the early explorers around the Canadian Arctic in waters that are still largely uncharted. Sarah Barrell went aboard.

Summer in the Arctic and dust, not snow, covers the ground. In Gjoa Haven, an Inuit settlement on King William, an island in the heart of the North-west Passage, there's dust on the seats of skidoos. Dust, too, on the coats of the scrappy sled dogs that are tethered in long lines waiting for winter and starter's orders.

About them, teenagers charge around on battered all-terrain vehicles, kicking up more dust, making the most of the light evenings and the comparatively balmy 10 °C temperatures. It's hard to imagine amid all this, with the sun shooting in laser-bright arcs off the town's tin-roofed houses, that somewhere in or around this island, Sir John Franklin, Britain's most intrepid 19th-century Arctic explorer, met a dark and icy end trying to discover the fabled North-west Passage.

He vanished more than a century and a half ago, but the fever to find the remains of Franklin's expedition still runs high in the remote Canadian Arctic, some 5000 kilometres from British shores. Earlier this summer, Canadian authorities unveiled the wreck of HMS *Investigator*, one of the many doomed 19th-century rescue ships sent in search of Franklin's expedition. Then, just last week in the town of Gjoa Haven itself, archaeologists unearthed what could be the Holy Grail of Arctic exploration history. At the behest of local brothers Wally and Andrew Porter, a box was excavated containing, the Porters claim, long sought-after records from the ill-fated Franklin expedition that might reveal its final whereabouts.

He was old, overweight and his ships spectacularly over-burdened when Franklin left for his third Arctic expedition in 1845. The British Admiralty brushed this aside as the fervour to conquer the North-west Passage once again reached a peak. There was prize money at stake (£20 000 [USD 28 000] offered by the British crown) for anyone who could navigate the elusive, icy waterway connecting the Atlantic and Pacific oceans. But beyond this, there was the chance to forge crucial northern trade links between Europe and the Orient, one that would open up a new route to the spice lands and, in addition, avoid stormy sailings around Cape Horn. But was Franklin the man to fly Britain's flag into the uncharted north?

Probably not, given that he had survived his first expedition charting Canada's Arctic coast by eating his own boots and being rescued by Native Americans. There was much that European explorers could learn from the three centuries of sailors who had battled to find a northerly route connecting the Atlantic and Pacific – in short, to travel light and use local expertise. Instead, highlighting the egotism of the time, Franklin's expedition sailed out of London laden with chests of fine china, dead-weight sledges and canned food that would later finish them off with lead-poisoning. After three winters trapped in ice, Franklin's crew abandoned their two ships, the *Erebus* and *Terror*, somewhere off the coast of King William Island and were never seen again. →

→

I manage to stop at this remote part of the Arctic Archipelago on board an eight-day tour, uniquely led by a local Inuit team. In true expedition style, there are no promised ports of call as conditions can change suddenly. Our first two days' passage is devoid of ice or high seas, but we hear that another cruise ship has run aground in shallow straits to the far west. 'Even with the ice receding, there's only been clear passage here for about five years,' says Dugald Wells, President of Cruise North, a former marine engineer who has been working in the Arctic since the mid-1980s. 'I came up here because it was fun – a real frontier. It still is, but you have to respect the fact that only 50 per cent of these waters are surveyed,' he says.

From *The Independent*, 19 September 2010

1 Imagine that you are Sarah Barrell, the writer of this article. On your return from your trip, you have been invited to give a talk to a group of Cambridge IGCSE students at a school in your home town. Write the words of your talk. You should include:

- information about Franklin and the search for the North-west Passage

- details of the area of the Arctic that you visited

- what you found particularly interesting and enjoyable about your trip and why you recommend people in your audience to visit the area at some point in their lives.

....

....

....

....

....

....

....

....

....

....

....

2 On her return from her visit to the Arctic, Sarah Barrell is interviewed on a local radio station about her experiences. Write the words of the conversation between Sarah and the interviewer. The interviewer asks these three main questions during the course of the interview:

- Tell me about Sir John Franklin and your interest in his journey.

- Were there any other reasons for your visit to the Arctic?

- What did you learn from your trip?

....

....

....

....

....

....

....

Photocopying prohibited

Cambridge IGCSE™ First Language English Workbook 2nd edition

Exercise 2

Read the following article carefully and then answer the questions which follow.

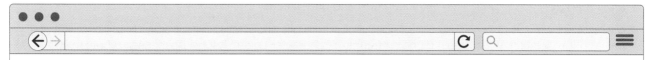

Experience: I was swept away by a flood

Vanessa Glover

'Shocked, tossed and buffeted, I gasped for breath and tried to keep my head above water.'

It was after midnight last December and we were driving home from a party. There had been extremely heavy rain on our journey there, though not enough to make us worry about the drive back. We were in our pick-up truck, which always felt safe. Paul, my husband, was driving and my seven-year-old son, Silas, was in the back.

What was so frightening was the speed of it. One minute we were halfway home and driving up to a familiar bridge, the next there was water rising over the bonnet. Deep floodwater was coursing across from a nearby railway line and surrounding fields, and we were caught in the middle of it.

The volume of water lifted our car up and pushed it back against a hedge. We were silent; I felt over-awed by the power of the water, and Paul was trying to control the truck.

Water was instantly around my ankles. I reached my hand back and felt it around Silas's, too. Paul climbed out through a window, at which point Silas woke up, confused and disoriented. I managed to pass him through the window to Paul, who was now on the truck's roof.

Paul told me I needed to get out, but I couldn't open my door or window. I managed to push my body though the driver's window and was left clinging onto the support between the windows. I was terrified the truck would capsize, pinning me beneath. Paul was incredulous, asking me what I was doing in the water, and telling me I needed to climb onto the bonnet, but I couldn't reach.

He grabbed my hood to help, but I could hear Silas crying, so I told him to let go – Silas needed him. He refused, but I insisted – I wanted to know Silas would be OK. As I saw his empty, outstretched hand, the water took me away. I'm a strong swimmer, but had no option but to shoot down the rapids. Shocked, tossed and buffeted, I gasped for breath and tried to keep my head above water. There was a horrendously loud noise, like a huge wall of bubbles swirling in my ears. I never expected to die of drowning.

I was washed over a garden wall into the river, 3.5 m higher than normal and flowing at about 23 kph. It was extremely dark but I could just make out trees. I reached out and grabbed two branches no bigger than my index finger, with a perfect tight grip. Somehow my feet wedged in a firm foothold and I hugged the tree with my knees. Another minute, and I'd have been sucked beneath a railway bridge.

My plan was just to hold on. My body went into shock a few times and I trembled involuntarily. I told myself it was a natural response and concentrated on not losing my foothold. Not knowing if Paul and Silas were dead or alive, I thought that if they survived they would need me.

After nearly 40 minutes, I saw a small spotlight. I shouted for help. Someone glimpsed my movement and a firefighter tried to talk to me, but I couldn't hear her above the roar of the water.

The light of a helicopter made me out in the tree. Their heat-seeking equipment had traced me, but they could see I had no warmth in my lower body and were concerned I would become hypothermic and lose my grip. My husband, who had been rescued with my son in the bucket of a mechanical digger, was nearby with a policewoman. She reassured him that so long as they could hear me, there was hope.

→

→

Guided to me by the helicopter, the rescue team managed to steer the boat to my shoulder. Four strong arms lifted me into the boat and I felt sheer relief and utter safety.

My rescuers were volunteers who have since received medals and I have an incredibly deep bond with them. In the isolation of that tree, I found a strength of character I didn't know I possessed – but I'm still flabbergasted I survived at all.

Adapted from *The Guardian*, 15 June 2013

1 On the day after their rescue, Vanessa and her family were interviewed by a national newspaper. Imagine that you are the journalist who conducted the interview. Write an article with the headline 'Family's Nightmare Flood Experience'. In your article you should include:

- what you learnt from interviewing Vanessa about her experience
- what you learnt when you interviewed Paul and Silas about their experiences
- any suggestions you have that would help other people cope in similar circumstances.

....

....

....

....

....

....

....

....

....

....

....

....

....

....

....

....

....

....

....

....

....

2 Imagine that you are Vanessa. After you have recovered from your ordeal in the flood, you write a letter to your sister, who lives in a different country, about your experience. In your letter you should include:

- details of the evening before the flood and how the flood occurred
- an account of your experience during the flood and how you and your family survived
- your thoughts and feelings both during the experience and now that you are safe at home.

....

....

....

....

....

....

....

....

....

....

....

....

....

....

....

....

....

....

....

....

....

....

3 Imagine that you were the lead firefighter during the rescue of Vanessa and her family. You have to write a report for the authorities on what happened during that night. Write your report under the following headings:

- Causes of the event and circumstances leading up to the rescue

- Actions of the firefighters and other rescue agencies

- Particular problems encountered and recommendations for the future

....

....

....

....

....

Exercise 3

The following passage is an extract from the short story 'The Country of the Blind' by H.G. Wells. Nunez, an explorer in the Andes mountain range in South America, has fallen down a mountainside onto a rocky ledge where he has spent the night. Read the passage carefully and then answer the questions which follow.

He was awakened by the singing of birds in the trees far below.

He sat up and perceived he was at the foot of a vast precipice. Over against him another wall of rock reared itself against the sky. The gorge between these precipices ran east and west. It was full of the morning sunlight, which lit the mass of fallen mountain to the west. Below him it seemed there was a precipice equally steep, but behind the snow in the gully he found a sort of chimney-cleft dripping with snow-water, down which a desperate man might venture. He found it easier than it seemed and after a rock climb of no particular difficulty came to a steep slope of trees. He turned his face up the gorge and saw it opened out above onto green meadows, among which he glimpsed a cluster of stone huts of unfamiliar fashion. At times his progress was like clambering along the face of a wall, and after a time the rising sun ceased to strike along the gorge, the voices of the singing birds died away, and the air grew cold and dark about him. But the distant valley with its houses was all the brighter for that. Among the rocks he noted an unfamiliar fern. He picked a frond or so and gnawed its stalk, and found it helpful.

About midday he came at last out of the gorge into the plain and the sunlight. He was stiff and weary; he sat down in the shadow of a rock, filled up his flask with water from a spring and drank it down. He remained for a time, resting before he went on to the houses.

They were very strange to his eyes, and indeed the whole appearance of that valley became, as he regarded it, stranger and more unfamiliar. The greater part of its surface was lush green meadow, starred with many beautiful flowers. It was irrigated with extraordinary care, and showed signs of systematic farming. High up and ringing the valley about was a wall, and what appeared to be a water channel, from which the little trickles of water that fed the meadow plants came. On the higher slopes flocks of llamas cropped the scanty grass. The irrigation streams ran together into a main channel down the centre of the valley, and this was enclosed on either side by a wall chest high. A number of paths paved with black and white stones, and each with a curious little kerb at the side, ran here and there in an orderly manner.

The houses of the central village were quite unlike those of the mountain villages he knew. They stood in a continuous row on either side of a central street of astonishing cleanness. Here and there their walls were pierced by a door, but not a solitary window broke their even frontage. They were parti-coloured with extraordinary irregularity, smeared with a sort of plaster that was sometimes grey, sometimes drab, sometimes slate-coloured or dark brown. It was the sight of this wild plastering that made the explorer say to himself, 'The good man who did that must have been as blind as a bat.'

He descended a steep place, and so came to the wall and channel that ran about the valley. He could now see a number of men and women resting on piled heaps of grass, as if taking a siesta, in the remoter part of the meadow. Nearer the village a number of children were lying on their backs, and then coming closer to him he saw three men. These men wore garments of llama cloth and boots and belts of leather, and caps of cloth with back and ear flaps. They followed one another in single file, walking slowly and yawning as they walked, like men who have been up all night. There was something so reassuringly prosperous and respectable in their bearing that after a moment's hesitation Nunez stood forward as conspicuously as possible upon his rock, and gave vent to a mighty shout that echoed round the valley.

From 'The Country of the Blind' by H.G. Wells

1 Imagine that you are Nunez. It is the day after the events described in the passage. You are now resting in the village and writing up the events of the previous days in your journal. In your journal entry you should include:

- an account of how you came to find the valley and the village
- what your first impressions of the village were
- what happened after you entered the village and met the inhabitants.

....

....

....

....

....

....

2 You are a journalist working for the magazine *Travellers' Tales*. A man called Nunez has contacted you and said that he has just returned from an unusual experience in the Andes. You interview him and then write an account of his experiences for the magazine. Your article is entitled 'Secrets of the Hidden Village' and it should include:

- information about Nunez and a description of his character

- details of how he discovered the village

- what he told you about the people he met and the time he spent with them.

....

....

....

....

....

....

....

....

....

....

....

Exercise 4

The following article is about the apparent sightings of mysterious creatures in Siberia in 2012. Read the article and then answer the questions which follow.

They just rushed away, all in fur, walking on two legs: Three yeti 'sightings' in Siberia in a week

Will Stewart

Three separate 'sightings' of yetis have been made in Siberia in recent weeks, say fishermen and an official in Russia. All were in the remote Kemerovo region, where around 30 'abominable snowmen' live, according to the country's leading researcher on the creatures.

In one previously undisclosed case last month near Myski village, fishermen in a boat on a river initially mistook distant figures first for bears and then people, said the *Siberian Times*.

'We shouted to them – do you need help?' said fisherman Vitaly Vershinin.

'They just rushed away, all in fur, walking on two legs, making their way through the bushes and with two other limbs, straight up the hill.'

He said: 'What did we think? It could not be bears, as the bear walks on all-fours, and they ran on two ... so then they were gone.'

In a second sighting on the bank of the Mras-Su River several days later, an unnamed fisherman was quoted saying: 'We saw some tall animals looking like people.'

He added: 'Our binoculars were broken and did not let us see them sharply. We waved at the animals but they did not respond, then quickly ran back into the forest, walking on two legs.

'We realised that they were not in dark clothes but covered by dark fur. They did walk like people.'

In a further case this month, an unnamed forestry inspector had encountered a 'yeti' in Shorsky National Park, according to local government official Sergei Adlyakov.

'The creature did not look like a bear and quickly disappeared after breaking some branches of the bushes,' he said.

No images have appeared from the alleged sightings.

Russia's leading 'yeti' expert, Igor Burtsev, said the 'sighting' was 'significant' though he was unaware of the later Shorsky National Park case.

He added: 'We shall explore new areas, to the north from the usual places yetis have been seen previously. The conference will start in Moscow and then we will travel with our guests to Kemerovo region.'

On a similar expedition last year, he claimed to have found yeti hair though no DNA findings have been released. He claims the creature – also known as Bigfoot and Sasquatch – is the missing link between Neanderthal man and modern human beings.

Burtsev has previously claimed a population of around 30 yetis are living in Kemerovo region.

'We have good evidence of the yeti living in our region, and we have heard convincing details from experts elsewhere in Russia and in the US and Canada,' he said. 'The descriptions of the habits of the Abominable Snowmen are similar from all over the world.'

Last November hunters claimed they had discovered the nest of a legendary yeti in the same area of Siberia. Experts stumbled across trees, twisted by force to form an arch, in the area which is famed for sightings of the wildman.

Biologist John Bindernagel, 69, said: 'We didn't feel like the trees we saw in Siberia had been done by a man or another mammal.'

→

'Twisted trees like this have also been observed in North America and they could fit in with the theory that Bigfoot makes nests.'

Sightings of the yeti have been reported in France, North America and the Himalayas but Dr Bindernagel said these are mainly ignored by scientists who are put off by 'jokes and taboos'.

Mr Burtsev has previously strongly denied accusations that yeti 'sightings' are a bizarre ruse to attract tourists to the far-flung region.

Reports say the two-legged creatures are heavy-set, around 7 ft tall and resemble bears.

Still at large: The history of the yeti

The first accounts of yetis emerged before the 19th century from Buddhists who believed that the creature inhabited the Himalayas.

They depicted the mysterious beast as having similarities to an ape and carrying a large stone as a weapon while making a whistling sound.

Popular interest in the creature gathered pace in the early 20th century as tourists began making their own trips to the region to try and capture the yeti. They reported seeing strange markings in the snow.

The *Daily Mail* newspaper led a trip called the Snowman Expedition in 1954 to Everest. During the trip, mountaineering leader John Angelo Jackson photographed ancient paintings of yetis and large footprints in the snow. A number of hair samples were also found that were believed to have come from a yeti scalp.

British mountaineer Don Whillans claimed to have witnessed a creature when scaling Annapurna in 1970.

Adapted from the *Daily Mail*, 23 September 2012

1   Imagine that you are Igor Burtsev. You have now had time to study the accounts of both yeti sightings. You have been asked to prepare a report for the other delegates at the Moscow conference. In your report you should refer to:

- what you have learnt from the people who witnessed the most recent sightings of the yetis

- how their accounts are similar to and different from earlier accounts of yeti sightings

- your reasons for believing that yetis do exist and reasons why other people might believe that they do not exist.

....

....

....

....

....

....

....

....

....

....

....

....

....

....

....

....

....

....

....

2 You are a presenter of a popular science television programme. As part of a feature about unexplained phenomena, you are interviewing John Bindernagel about stories concerning yetis and other similar creatures. Write the words of your conversation. As the interviewer, you ask the following three main questions:

- Could you tell the viewers about some of the most interesting sightings of yetis and other similar creatures?

- What theories have been developed as to why yetis might exist?

- What reasons do you have for thinking that we should seriously believe or not believe in the existence of yetis?

....

....

....

....

Exercise 5

In the following passage a journalist, Giles Tremlett, reflects satirically on the opening of one of the tallest hotels in Benidorm, a popular holiday resort on Spain's Costa Blanca. Read the passage and then answer the questions which follow.

Benidorm gets high and mighty ugly

Giles Tremlett

Resort hopes the tallest hotel in Europe will add to its 5m visitors.

It was life as normal in the cafes and bars dedicated to keeping Benidorm's legion of tourists happy last night. Fish and chips and all-day British breakfasts were on sale and there was the promise of Sky Sport or karaoke later in the evening.

But the talk was not about soccer or television programmes. Instead it was of their latest neighbour, a giant hotel which, even by the brash standards of Europe's tackiest resort, promises to take British package tourism to new heights.

Those who stepped outside inevitably found themselves craning their necks upwards and staring at the neon-lit superstructure of the concrete and glass Gran Bali Hotel – the newest addition to a skyline already bristling with ugly skyscrapers – which opened its doors yesterday. At 48 floors, it has the dubious distinction of being the tallest hotel in Europe.

'What happens if it is bombed? We will all die,' muttered one worried Bridewell drinker.

At 186 metres tall, the glitzy, garish Bali is Europe's 13th largest skyscraper. Its presence here confirms Benidorm's status as the high-rise tourism capital of the world.

Some 1500 holidaymakers at a time will squeeze into the Bali's 778 rooms, together with several hundred more who already stay at a smaller hotel on the same site. Eighteen lifts, including two on the outside of the building, will send them hurtling backwards and forwards to their rooms.

Guests can have their wrinkles zapped by lasers, get their blonde streaks redone or tan themselves by the pool while enjoying a view of the neighbouring skyscrapers that populate this concrete oasis.

Fake mountain waterfalls make a vain attempt at reminding visitors of the real tropical paradise that gave the hotel its name. Jacuzzis and 150 m high sun decks are on offer to those prepared to take the most luxurious penthouse suites.

The owners, who dream of turning Benidorm into a Mediterranean Las Vegas, are lobbying for a new gambling law to be passed so that they can also offer their guests the joys of one-armed bandits, blackjack and roulette wheels.

'I am proud. This is the start of a new era for Benidorm,' explained Joaquin Perez, one of the co-owners. 'Soon we will have more hotel beds here than even London or Paris. We must bring people from all over the world.'

More than five million visitors a year is not enough for Benidorm, despite the elbow-room-only crowds in its old town or the battle for sunloungers on its beaches. The Bali is just part of a plan to add 10 000 holiday beds to the 50 000 plus already here within the next two years.

Special deals with package tour companies mean that many of the rooms at the Bali will be taken by some of the 1.2 million British tourists who come here every year. Elton John was expected to be the first of what the management hopes will be many showbiz guests to cast some glamour on the town's tawdry reputation. His glitzy style is just what the new Benidorm wants.

→

→

British tourists who went to gaze at the Bali yesterday were sceptical. 'I wouldn't stay up there,' said Lynn Hall from Manchester.

'Our tour rep said there were rumours that it was either sinking or beginning to lean over.'

The Bali is at its most spectacular at night, and from a distance, when it looks like a massive, silver knife, projecting beams of light up into the clouds. By day it becomes a dull, grey, concrete and glass giant, visible for many kilometres. 'We kept waiting for them to paint it,' said one local.

Town authorities denied that the resort, which already has to recycle its water, had reached saturation point. 'Benidorm will now have to grow upwards, just like this,' said the town-hall spokeswoman. 'Anyone who insults the five million people who come here every year is insulting the ordinary people of Europe,' she told reporters. 'Benidorm is just one of those places that you either love or hate.'

Its newest building is no exception to that rule.

Adapted from *The Guardian*, 18 May 2002

1 You are a representative of Benidorm's town council at the time when plans for the Gran Bali Hotel are being discussed before the hotel is built. You have been asked to give a speech at a public meeting attended by people who are concerned about the effect of the building on the town. Write the words of your speech. You should include:

- the reasons that you understand why some people may object to the building of the hotel
- details of what the planned hotel will look like and the facilities it will offer
- your reasons for thinking that the hotel will offer great benefits to the town of Benidorm.

....

....

....

....

....

....

....

....

....

....

....

....

....

....

....

....

....

....

....

2 You are a journalist for a travel magazine. The Gran Bali Hotel has now been open and fully functioning for a year and you have just spent a short break there. Write an article for your magazine about your experiences in Benidorm. You should include:

- a brief account of the controversy over the building of the hotel

- details of the hotel itself and what it offers to its typical guests

- your reasons for recommending, or not recommending, that your readers both visit Benidorm and stay in the Gran Bali Hotel while they are there.

....

....

....

....

....

....

....

Exercise 6

In the following passage, the writer Andrew Leonard describes how, while on holiday on the island of Kauai, he finally managed to escape from his computer and all the other electronic gadgets that control his life when he is at work. Read the passage and then answer the questions which follow.

Unplugged: A peaceful holiday

Andrew Leonard

After bouncing my rental car across several kilometres of red-dirt cane roads I walked for nearly another kilometre down the beach to a deserted cove. It was comforting to think that at the very least I was finally out of cell-phone range.

However, even on Kauai, Hawaii's 'Garden Island', complete escape wasn't all that easy to achieve. Noisy helicopters full of tourists buzzed and darted overhead like so many dragonflies. Every 20 minutes or so the soothing sounds of wind and water were broken by the rumble of a speeding tour boat racing to complete another lap around the island. Worst of all, not more than five minutes by car from the resort where I was staying, the Atomic Clock Internet Cafe beckoned with promises of instant email.

I felt uncomfortable every time I drove by the Atomic Clock Cafe. I am a technology reporter for an online magazine – my life is driven and dominated by email. I'm drowned in it, usually 400 or 500 messages a day. The main reason for my visit to Kauai was to unplug, disconnect, log off, and get away from it all. No cell phone, no electronic organiser, no laptop. And definitely no email.

Yes, my plan was to lie on the beach and not check my email. My friends and family were outraged as they could not understand how I could bear to live without email. But they didn't understand. In my job, I am online, permanently. Cyberspace is more familiar to me than my backyard. While I am awake, my email is always on. I don't like to be without it for too long.

A few hours away from it, and I start to shiver.

I am, however, no stranger to beaches and their relaxing qualities and so I knew, even when arriving well after dark at the comfortable cottage in the town of Waimea, that the island of Kauai gave me a good chance of beating my addiction to electronic gadgets.

Maybe it was the full moon illuminating the black-sand beach not 10 metres from my door. Or the mango trees casting shadows across the veranda. Or the driftwood piled in loose heaps for as far as I could see along the shore. Without question, the long, slow sound of the waves rolling in calmed my restless soul, and I found I could, in fact, log off.

That accomplished, the next morning I turned to the second part of my plan. The island offered all varieties of beach pleasures: bodysurfing beaches, wading beaches, secluded beaches. There were also classic South Pacific semicircular beaches of white sand lined with palm trees that stretched ahead. Black sand, white sand, brown sand, sugar sand … I could hike 20 kilometres to the far-away isolation of Kauai, drive a sport-utility vehicle onto Polihale Beach, or stroll from some hotel into the welcoming waters at Kalapaki or Poipu.

After looking at a few guidebooks, I began to feel worried. So many beaches, so little time! I planned ways to pack in as many different beaches as possible into a single afternoon. What would be most efficient, I wondered – driving north to Hanelei Bay and working my way south? Or just picking out one specific beach?

But then I thought again. Going to the beach should not be about efficiency. That's the world of email – the world I was leaving behind. Forget efficiency. The beach, after all, wasn't about satisfying immediate urges. The beach was about surrendering to the *lack* of urgency.

→

At my cottage, I finally found myself sitting motionless in my chair, book closed on my lap, a drink untouched by my side, idly watching a lizard skitter across the ceiling. That evening, staring with pleasure at the sun sinking slowly beneath the waves, I discovered that I wasn't in the least bit alarmed when a gentle shower of rain came down on me. No matter – whether I was wet, dry, on the sand, in the water – the beach had a way of making time non-existent. On the beach I could wait for the coconut to fall; I didn't need to shake the tree.

Adapted from www.islands.com/article/Unplugged

1 Imagine that you are Andrew Leonard. It is the evening of the fifth day of your holiday and you are sitting in your cottage writing your journal. In your journal entry you should include:

- details of what you have spent your time doing while you have been on Kauai

- what you have found most pleasing about your time on the island and about the island itself

- your thoughts on not using any electronic gadgets and how this might change your outlook when you return to work.

....

....

....

....

....

....

....

....

....

....

....

....

....

2 You are a journalist for the local Kauai newspaper and have recently interviewed Andrew Leonard during his time on the island. Write an article with the headline 'The Man For Whom Time Stood Still'. In your article you should include:

- your impressions of Andrew as a person and his reasons for visiting Kauai

- how he has found life without electronic devices and what problems this has caused him

- how far Andrew feels that Kauai fulfils his idea of an ideal getaway and whether he thinks future visitors will be able to have the same experiences that he has had.

....

....

....

....

....

....

....

....

....

....

....

....

....

....

....

3 Imagine that you are Andrew Leonard. It has been two days since you first arrived on Kauai and you realise that your friends will be wondering how you are getting on. Write a letter to one of your friends at work. In your letter you should include:

- your first impressions of Kauai, what you have been doing since you arrived and what you plan to do for the remainder of your holiday

- how you are coping without email and other electronic devices, and why your friend would benefit from doing something similar

- for how long you think that Kauai will remain unspoilt by outside influences.

Directed writing exercises

As mentioned at the start of this section, the directed writing tasks require you to respond by writing in either a discursive or an argumentative way.

Exercise 7

Read carefully these two passages about the ways in which mobile phone use can involve a potential threat to our personal freedom. Then answer the question which follows.

Note

For each practice question which follows, you should base your response on what you have read in the passages but you should not copy from them. You should attempt to use your own words throughout. Your answer should address and develop all three points in the question. You should write 250–350 words.

Mobile phone users' movements 'could be sold for profit'

Hackers could steal users' location data, finding out 'where you are, how you got there and where you are going', say campaigners.

Mobile phone users are one data breach away from having the routines of their daily lives revealed to criminals, privacy campaigners have said.

Mobile phone networks and wireless hotspot operators are collecting detailed information on customers' movements that reveal intimate details of their lives, two separate investigations into mobile data retention have found.

Many people unwittingly sign up to be location-tracked 24/7, unaware that the highly sensitive data this generates is being used and sold on for profit. Campaigners say that if this information were stolen by hackers, criminals could use it to target children as they leave school or homes after occupants have gone out.

It is so detailed that it can reveal customers' gender, religion and many other personal details that could present serious risks of blackmail.

'Effectively, consumers are opting in to being location tracked by default,' said a member of Krowdthink, the privacy campaign group behind one of the investigations.

'The fact of the matter is your mobile service provider knows – without you knowing – where you are, how you got there and can figure out where you are going.'

'Such precise location data would be like 'gold dust' for criminals if it found its way on to the black market,' said Pete Woodward, of security experts Securious.

'The information that mobile and Wi-Fi service providers hold on location tracking is an evolving and high-risk area of cybercrime that needs urgent attention by the industry,' Woodward said. 'Otherwise we will face the frightening prospect that such highly sensitive data could get into the hands of the likes of kidnappers and other blackmailers.'

Krowdthink's research found that 93% of those questioned had opted in to location tracking, giving mobile phone and wireless operators unlimited access to their whereabouts 24 hours a day. This data, the report says, connects web users' digital lives with their physical lives, making it one of the most intrusive forms of tracking.

Yet this research has found that customers were not being given clear enough information about how the data is used, or opportunities to opt out of collection.

Adapted from https://www.theguardian.com/world/2016/apr/04/mobile-phone-users-
movements-are-tracked-and-sold-for-profit

The end of privacy?

Pete Warren

Forget Street View, there is a far more subtle – and pervasive – invasion of your private life being carried out – this time through your mobile phone.

Each time you use your phone, data on your habits is stored and could be sold to advertisers.

The mobile phone industry has for years seen the potential for a rich market to develop in location-based services if only it could get its customers to agree.

The industry's aim is to unite information on customers' age, gender, web-browsing habits, home address and buying patterns with a record of their daily movements, and subject that to behavioural analysis techniques.

This provides data on you – the customer – so powerful that the companies involved can predict what you are about to do next, and then sell that information to brands interested in marketing to you.

'What is going on at the moment is the opening of a barn door into your personal habits,' says Glyn Read, a former marketing director of SAS Institute, a leading behavioural analysis company.

'The value of understanding people's personal information is enormous – this will allow a form of subliminal advertising to develop,' says Read, adding: 'We are at the tip of an iceberg of what is possible. The real worry comes when governments start to demand access to this data.'

Read's comments are confirmed by Laurie Miles, head of analytics for SAS UK. 'We have been working with all of the big banks and with the mobile industry on what can be achieved from mobile data,' he says. 'We can also collect data from people's voices to tell whether they are lying or not, so this gives us an opportunity to bring marketing and risk together.'

Up till now, the mobile phone industry has always had that information, but data protection rules have stopped it being used because their customers have not given permission for them to do so.

While the mobile industry are adamant nothing can happen without the customer's permission, users may not realise what they are agreeing to. If you sign up for many services with some companies, you are unlikely to realise you are giving permission for all of your data to be used for marketing.

But this position is not good enough for the campaign group Privacy International. 'This is a catastrophic corruption of consent. People are being told that they are signing up for marketing when in fact they are being opted into a massive surveillance strategy,' says Simon Davies, director of Privacy International.

Glyn Read goes even further: 'People do not realise the huge potential of this information for controlling our lives. We are sleepwalking into a minefield.'

Adapted from *The Guardian*, 2 April 2009

2 DIRECTED WRITING

You are very concerned about the threat to our privacy which may result from our use of mobile phones and are determined to make others aware of this danger. You ask your teacher if you can talk about your concerns to your class as one of your speaking and listening tasks. Your teacher agrees. Write the words of your talk in which you explain:

- what the dangers are and how they have arisen

- why recent developments are increasing the threats to our personal privacy

- what you think should be done and how you and your friends can try to improve matters.

Exercise 8

Read these two passages carefully and then answer the question which follows. The first passage was written by a journalist about her personal experiences of eating. The second passage is taken from the website of the animal rights organisation Animal Aid.

'Delicious!'

Rachael Oliveck was a committed vegetarian and animal rights activist for 14 years. But on Christmas Day she finally cracked, and tucked into some turkey – and she hasn't looked back since.

It wasn't specifically the thought of roast turkey that changed my mind, but this year's Christmas dinner was notable for marking the moment I gave up vegetarianism after fourteen long, virtuous years. And, to save me answering the same three questions over and over again – yes, it was delicious, no, my body didn't seize up in shock and, yes, I have eaten meat at least once a day since.

I originally gave up meat for ethical reasons, and have always missed the taste of it. As an animal rights activist, I was primarily concerned about the conditions of animals reared for meat, and I was also put off by the routine feeding of antibiotics and growth hormones to livestock.

In 1989 these were not widely understood views, and spreading the word on animal cruelty was perceived as scaremongering at best and downright unnatural at worst. Being vegetarian was solely the preserve of the crank, hippy and the misguided but well-intentioned teenage girl. Supermarkets stocked 'veggie grills' (yellowish, cutlet-shaped minced vegetables) which were a barbecue staple in the summer, and restaurants routinely offered plates of vegetables as the meat-free option.

Since then, meat, and indeed food production, has changed enormously, as have eating habits in general. Humanely-reared meat is widely available, eating less meat is the norm, supermarkets offer huge veggie ranges and restaurants have wised up to what non-meat eaters want. Following the public furore surrounding BSE and, to a lesser extent, the foot-and-mouth outbreak, the horrors of modern meat production have become widely known, and vegetarians feel they have been proved right. Meat is now much more traceable and, it is hoped, of higher quality.

I wish I was noble enough to claim that it was simply a question of ethics. If I am honest, it was just as much a question of gluttony. I have always loved food, and I had taken to staring at the meat sections of my favourite cookery book and watching food programmes in a desperate attempt to satisfy a growing desire for the flesh of defenceless animals. Meat didn't repel me any more. I wanted to eat it. I realised that I was no longer taking a principled stand that I was proud of, I was simply missing out. My stomach may have been meat-free but, in my heart, I was a ravenous carnivore. And that was that.

I cannot imagine that I will ever go back to vegetarianism, but I used to think I would never eat meat again. I am hoping, however, that my diet will balance out, and I will be able to combine meat and meat-free. What is undeniable is that the physical effects of eating meat have been striking; I have more energy, feel much better and, according to friends, I look much healthier. I went back to meat for reasons of taste, but I am pretty sure that, had my choices been restricted to cheap, greyish cuts and mechanically recovered meat, I would have stuck with the vegetables and soya.

Some ethical principles remain – so far I have tried to buy humanely-reared meat wherever possible. I still find the idea of veal or foie gras distasteful, and doubt I will be tempted by them for some while yet. I don't feel as if I failed at vegetarianism, nor that I have condemned poor little animals to a life of unending misery just to satisfy my stomach.

Adapted from *The Guardian*, 29 January 2003

Is meat damaging the environment?

Animal farming is a major source of pollution and environmental destruction and is responsible for 14.5% of all greenhouse gas emissions – more than the entire transport sector. Intensive factory farming is one of the main causes of water pollution. Globally, farm animals reared to satisfy people's appetite for meat consume increasing quantities of water, land and food. Cattle ranching is also one of the main causes of tropical rainforest destruction.

Many of the world's fish species have been decimated because of over-fishing, and a lot of sea bird populations are now threatened because there are not enough fish for them to survive. Many sea creatures and birds are killed when they get caught up in discarded fishing tackle and drift nets.

Rearing animals for food is very wasteful. We can feed between four and ten times as many people on a vegetarian diet by growing crops directly for human consumption. In some countries, crops are exported for cattle food, and people in the exporting country starve!

Adapted from www.animalaid.org.uk

Your cousin, who lives in another town, is trying to decide whether or not to become vegetarian and has asked for your advice. This is a purely personal decision and there are no religious reasons influencing your cousin's decision. However, you know that your cousin is very concerned about the future of the environment and the ways in which human beings can cause damage to it.

You have no strong views either way about the subject of vegetarianism. Write a letter to your cousin in which you give reasons for and against the choice he or she is about to make. In your letter you should include:

• reasons for changing to a vegetarian diet

• reasons for continuing to eat meat

• what you think would be the most suitable choice for your cousin and your reasons for making this suggestion.

Photocopying prohibited

3 Writing summaries

Writing a summary

The purpose of writing a summary is to show evidence that you:

- have understood what you have read

- can select the relevant information

- can express the information using your own words and in a shorter form than the original passage.

The guidance which follows is a review of the advice about writing summaries given in the Student's Book. The points are given here to remind you of how you should approach summary writing tasks.

Step 1: Read the question carefully

This is very important, as it is unlikely that you will be required to summarise the whole of the original passage. The wording of the question will direct you towards the points you should include. For example, the whole passage may be about everyday life in Japan, but you may be asked to summarise only what it tells you about going to school in that country. You must, therefore, keep the wording of the question clearly in mind when reading the passage.

Step 2: Read right through the passage(s) once

This will allow you to gain a good overall understanding of what the material is about.

Step 3: Identify the information that is relevant

Refresh your memory of what the question asks you to do and then read through the passage again very carefully. At this stage you should underline or highlight on the question paper all the information that is relevant to the question. You must be ruthless. Ignore anything that is not relevant, no matter how interesting you may find it. It may help if you give your summary a title.

Step 4: Make notes

Now is the time to put pen to paper. You should make rough notes of the points you have identified, using your own words as far as possible.

Remember, the use of your own words is important as this is a way of showing that you have understood the passage(s). Try to:

- **paraphrase** (rephrase) parts of the text to which you refer

- use **synonyms** – words with the same meaning – instead of the exact words from the text.

This will make it very clear that you understand what you have read.

You do not have to use your own words when making notes but you may find that it will help when writing your final summary if you do so. You should make the notes in the space for planning your answer in the exam answer booklet but your plan will **not** be marked by an examiner.

Step 5: Count the main points

Once you have noted all the main points, count how many you have identified.

If you have identified 15 points and you are aiming to write a summary of about 150 words, then, as a rough guide, try to write about ten words for each point.

Step 6: Write the summary

Once you have written rough notes in your own words, you should write them up as a piece of continuous prose, trying to keep your expression as concise as possible. If your notes are sufficiently detailed, this may only be a fine-tuning job.

Step 7: Final check

Once you have written your summary, read it through to check that it makes sense. You may not have to count the number of words you wrote. If, for example, you know that you usually write about eight words per line, then a quick count up of the number of lines you have filled will give some indication of how many words you have written in total.

Summary writing is tested in Paper 1 of the Cambridge IGCSE™ First Language English examination. You will need to demonstrate your understanding of what you have read *and* your written expression. There are 10 marks available for reading and 5 marks for written expression. The reading marks are not necessarily awarded on a mark per point basis but will take into account the *range* of points you have made and how effectively they have been selected to give an overview of the main ideas of the passage that are relevant to the subject of the summary.

Marks for written expression will be awarded for your answer to the second part of the question, which requires you to write your own version of the summary in continuous prose. These marks are awarded primarily for the quality of your summary writing technique (for example, how focused your response is and how well you have expressed yourself concisely and in your own words). However, the technical accuracy of your written expression will also have some bearing on the marks awarded.

The passage for summary (Text B) will be about 350–400 words in length and your summary should not exceed 150 words.

Key points

It is important that you try to keep within the suggested word limit. A very long answer will almost certainly contain irrelevant material and repetition. An answer which is significantly less than the suggested number of words will have left out key points.

Remember, you must take time to read the passages carefully – in these questions, more marks are awarded for reading and understanding than are available for writing.

Summary writing exercises

Exercise 1

Read the following extract carefully and then answer the questions which follow.

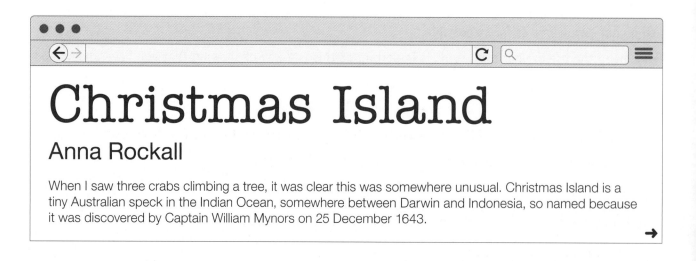

Christmas Island
Anna Rockall

When I saw three crabs climbing a tree, it was clear this was somewhere unusual. Christmas Island is a tiny Australian speck in the Indian Ocean, somewhere between Darwin and Indonesia, so named because it was discovered by Captain William Mynors on 25 December 1643.

→

Because it is one of the Earth's far-flung corners, it has a host of wildlife all of its own, and a few oddities that make it like another planet.

The first and foremost oddity is the crabs, found nowhere else in such numbers. They are found everywhere but the beach, for they are land-dwelling and, except in the breeding season, prefer the forest to the sea. There is also another kind of crab on the island, the monstrous robber crab, huge, ugly and frankly terrifying, which is a less commonly-found beast due to a small but persistent enemy – the 'crazy ants'.

The locally dubbed 'crazy ants' were carelessly imported sometime between the wars and found their perfect island with no predators. So they have indeed gone crazy. To walk through the jungle is to be permanently harassed by the little beasts trying to crawl up your legs.

So walking in the jungle seems like a good idea but isn't. And if the ants make life in the jungle uncomfortable for a walker, pity the giant robber crabs. They appear impenetrable, with their heavy armour and terrifying pincers that can crack coconut shells, but they are no match for the crazy ant. The ants may not be able to get through the crabs' thick shell, but they crawl up the stalks of their eyes and eat them.

The local insects that feed on rainforest trees have been luckier. The ants eat the honeydew they produce and in turn protect them against local predators such as wasps, spiders and parasites.

You don't even have to go to the jungle to see rare wildlife. Queuing outside the bank, I saw a fabulous gold pink bird with a long sweeping tail plonk itself idly in the car park; this was the magnificent golden bosun, which you will find nowhere else in the world, and which along with red crabs adorns the stamps and souvenirs of the island.

Adapted from *The Guardian*, 22 December 2001

1 Notes and planning

What do you learn about Christmas Island *and* the wildlife that can be found there from the passage? Use the space below to plan your answer.

2 Now write a summary of what the passage tells you about Christmas Island *and* the wildlife that can be found there. You should write no more than 150 words.

....

....

....

....

....

....

....

....

....

....

....

....

....

....

....

....

....

....

....

....

....

....

....

....

....

Exercise 2

Read the following extract carefully and then answer the questions which follow.

Mary Seacole was born in Kingston, Jamaica in 1805. Her father was a Scottish soldier, and her mother practised traditional Jamaican medicine and ran a small hostel in Jamaica where she cared for injured soldiers and their wives. Mary helped her mother and learned about medicine from her; she soon gained her own reputation as a 'skilful nurse'.

Mary travelled widely. In 1851, she joined her brother Edward in Panama, where she opened a hotel. Whilst she was there, she caught and recovered from cholera. She then gained extensive knowledge of the disease, and saved her first cholera patients.

She next travelled to London, where she heard about the Crimean War between Britain and Russia and how the nursing system there had collapsed. She applied to go to the Crimea to tend to the sick and wounded. She pointed out that she had wide experience, excellent references and knew many of the British soldiers and regiments. She had nursed them while they were stationed in Jamaica.

But she was rejected by everybody, including one of Florence Nightingale's assistants. 'Is it possible,' she asked herself, 'that people are not accepting my aid because my blood flows beneath a somewhat darker skin than theirs?' In her disappointment, Mary cried in the street.

A distant relative of hers, called Day, was going to the Crimea on business, and they agreed to start a general store and hotel called Seacole and Day, near the British Army camp. So, at the age of 50, with her large stock of medicines, Mary went to the battle zone. The moment she arrived there were sick and wounded to attend to. She opened her British hotel in the summer of 1855, near the city of Sevastopol. Soon the entire British Army knew of 'Mother Seacole'. The soldiers were her sons and she was their mother.

Though some of the army doctors had little respect for her work, others were more supportive. One army surgeon watched with admiration as she, numb with cold, looked after some soldiers, giving them tea and food and words of comfort. She was often on the front line and frequently under fire in the middle of the battle.

It was W.H. Russell, the first modern war correspondent, who made Mary Seacole's deeds in the Crimea famous. He described her as 'a warm and successful physician, who doctors and cures all manner of men with extraordinary success. She is always near the battle field ready to aid the wounded, and has earned many a poor soldier's blessings'.

Adapted from www.100greatblackbritons.com

1 Notes and planning

What do you learn about the life and actions of Mary Seacole *and* what different people thought about her from the passage? Use the space below to plan your answer.

2 Now write a summary of what the passage tells you about the life and actions of Mary Seacole *and* what different people thought about her. You should write no more than 150 words.

Exercise 3

Read the following extract carefully and then answer the questions which follow.

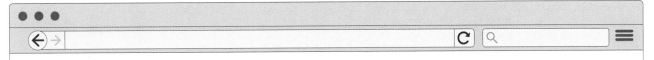

Mysteries of the sea

In April 2007, the 12-metre yacht, *Kaz II*, was found drifting 130 kilometres off the east Australian coastline, with no sign of its crew of three.

On board, the engine was running, the table was set for a meal and a computer was open and running. Apart from a torn sail, there were no signs of anything wrong on the boat. The crew have never been found, and no explanation has ever been given for their disappearance.

The yacht had set off three days before to sail around Northern Australia to Western Australia. Many theories have been advanced. The fact that fenders were down led to suggestions that *Kaz II* had been boarded by another boat and her crew were victims of foul play. As clothes were found neatly folded on the deck, another theory was that the three crew known to be on board had all taken a swim together. Other theories were that the yacht became stuck on a sandbank, and the men jumped overboard to push her free, but a gust of wind blew the vessel away from them, or that one fell overboard and the others were lost trying to save him. Instruments on board showed that the yacht had not been steered since the day of her departure; she had, therefore, been drifting for three full days before she was found. The mystery has never been solved.

Another mystery was that of the *Marie Celeste*, a large sailing vessel, discovered in the Atlantic Ocean in 1872, unmanned and under full sail, drifting towards Gibraltar. Of her people on board nothing has ever been learnt. She had sailed with a captain and a crew of seven, plus the captain's wife and two-year-old daughter.

The ship had set off on 5 November from New York, heading for Genoa. Just a month later, she was discovered drifting by another sailing ship, the *Dei Gratia*. The crew boarded the ship, finding her in generally good condition. One lifeboat had been launched, and the captain's instruments were missing. The *Marie Celeste* was world news at the time, but no conclusions were ever reached. Some suspicion fell on the crew of the *Dei Gratia* and they were rewarded only one fifth of what they should have received for bringing the ship home.

Adapted from www.sail-world.com/UK

1   Notes and planning

What do you learn about the *Kaz II* and the *Marie Celeste and* about what people think may have happened to them from the passage? Use the space below to plan your answer.

2 Now write a summary of what the passage tells you about the *Kaz II* and the *Marie Celeste and* about what people think may have happened to them. You should write no more than 150 words.

....

....

....

....

....

....

....

....

....

....

....

....

....

....

....

....

....

Exercise 4

Read the following extract carefully and then answer the questions which follow.

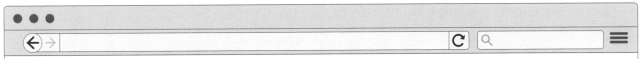

An early amusement park

The Vauxhall Pleasure Gardens (also known as Spring Gardens) were opened in 1661 and reached the height of their popularity in the early 1800s, with 20 000 visiting on one night in 1826. Their winning formula combined music, illuminated fountains, fireworks and light refreshments in an Eden-like atmosphere. The gardens originally combined genteel areas (where orchestras played and visitors promenaded in their finery) and 'dark walks' where couples could enjoy each other's company in some privacy, if not in comfort. This combination took some policing, and the owners employed their own policemen, probably the first organised police force in London.

Charles Dickens was not greatly impressed by the gardens' 'faded splendour' when he visited them in daylight in the 1830s: 'We walked about and met with a disappointment at every turn; our favourite views were mere patches of paint; the fountain that had sparkled so showily by lamplight presented very much the appearance of a water pipe that had burst; all the ornaments were dingy, and all the walks gloomy.'

Growing competition from early music halls and other public entertainments caused the proprietors to become increasingly innovative and offer a wider range of attractions, such as lion tamers and tightrope walkers. They were particularly famous for balloon ascents.

It was not particularly easy to get to Vauxhall – at least until Vauxhall Station was opened in 1848 mainly to service the gardens. The nearest Thames bridge was the often very congested London Bridge. But there were many boatmen willing to ferry passengers across and along the river, which was much slower moving than now.

London in fact had three particularly prominent pleasure gardens at Vauxhall, Marylebone and Ranelagh. They all thrived as a result of the prosperity of the 1700s, which in turn resulted from a relatively stable and democratic British Government and thriving international trade, much of it passing through London. As a result, many merchants and professionals found that they had the time and money to visit the opera and pleasure gardens, of which Vauxhall were the most fashionable. The Vauxhall Gardens therefore became a model for the Tivoli Gardens in Copenhagen, and numerous other pleasure gardens around the UK and Europe.

Vauxhall also gave the Russians their word for 'railway station', which is pronounced 'vokzal'. An article written by Lucien Tesnière in 1951 explains that the 'Vauxhall' at Pavlovsk was the destination of the first Russian railway line (from nearby St Petersburg) and so the word Vauxhall became synonymous with railway station.

There is, however, another unsubstantiated theory, which is that Vauxhall Station was visited in the late 1800s by a delegation sent to Britain by Tsar Nicholas I. The delegation learnt that Vauxhall, the last stop before Waterloo, was a ticket collecting point and perhaps thought that 'Vauxhall' meant this, rather than being a place name. Whatever the truth is, there is no question that Vauxhall Pleasure Gardens were certainly visited by Russians in the 19th century.

Thackeray, the novelist, extolled the virtues of the pleasure gardens in his book *Vanity Fair* (published in 1848), although they had by then begun to acquire an unsavoury reputation. Ironically, the advent of the railways killed off the gardens and they closed in 1859. The site was subsequently built upon and the present-day Spring Gardens now occupy part of the original site.

Adapted from www.vauxhallandkennington.org.uk

1   Notes and planning

What have you learnt from the passage about the history and reputation of the Vauxhall Pleasure Gardens *and* about the entertainment they provided? Use the space below to plan your answer.

2   Now write a summary of what the passage tells you about the history and reputation of the Vauxhall Pleasure Gardens *and* about the entertainment they provided. You should write no more than 200 words.

....

....

....

....

....

....

....

....

....

Exercise 5

Read the following extract carefully and then answer the questions which follow.

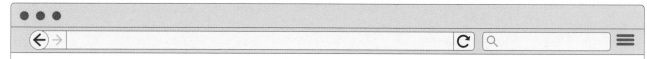

Deep sea discovery: The monsters from the deep

It is one of the most mysterious creatures of the deep ocean, and one of the most elusive. Only half a dozen colossal squid have been caught. The specimen hauled out of the inky waters of Antarctica is believed to be the biggest, weighing half a tonne, with eyes as big as dinner plates.

The gigantic sea creature, about 12 metres long, with a large beak and razor-sharp hooks on the end of its tentacles, was feasting on a Patagonian toothfish – itself one of the more sizeable members of the marine population – when it was caught by New Zealand fishermen this month.

Experts described it yesterday as a 'phenomenal' find. One said that if calamari rings were made from it, they would be the size of tractor tyres.

Colossal squid, or *Mesonychoteuthis hamiltoni*, are not related to giant squid, which grow to a maximum of 'only' 12 metres and are somewhat lighter. The biggest colossal squid are believed to reach 14 metres in length. They are active and aggressive killers that have been known to attack sperm whales, and they live at depths of up to 2000 metres.

The New Zealand Fisheries Minister, Jim Anderton, who announced the discovery of the new specimen, said it took fishermen two hours to land it. They had been fishing with long lines for Patagonian toothfish, also known as Chilean seabass, in the Southern Ocean. Mr Anderton said that 'the squid was eating a hooked toothfish when it was hauled from the deep.'

The crew stopped long lining and manoeuvred the squid into a cargo net to haul it on board their ship, *San Aspiring*. It was then frozen in the ship's hull and brought back to New Zealand for scientific analysis. Experts have yet to examine it, but they believe it to be the first intact adult male ever landed.

The species was first recorded in 1925, when two arms were found in the stomach of a sperm whale. In 1981, a Russian trawler caught a 4-metre immature female in its net in Antarctic waters. Another complete specimen was captured near the surface in 2003. But so few adults have been seen that scientists know next to nothing about the colossal squid's life history, diet, behaviour and reproductive patterns.

If initial estimates are correct, the 450-kg creature that is on its way to New Zealand's National Museum in Wellington, Te Papa, is 150 kg bigger than an immature female caught on the surface of the Ross Sea, off the Antarctic.

Steve O'Shea, a squid expert at Auckland University of Technology, said that the new specimen eclipsed that find. 'I can assure you that this is going to draw phenomenal interest,' he said. 'It is truly amazing.'

Mr Anderton predicted that marine scientists 'will be very interested in this amazing creature, as it adds immeasurably to our understanding of the marine environment'.

'The squid was almost dead when it reached the surface, and the careful work of the crew was paramount in getting this specimen aboard in good condition,' he said. 'The creature will be photographed, measured, tissue sampled, registered, and preserved intact for scientific study. Ongoing examination of this giant will help to unlock some of the mysteries of the deep ocean. Even answers to basic questions such as how large does this species grow to, and how long does it live for are not yet known.'

→

→

While colossal squid live in freezing Antarctic waters, giant squid, or *Architeuthis dux*, are found around the coast of New Zealand. Dr O'Shea has described colossal squid as 'not just larger, but an order of magnitude meaner'. He told the BBC: 'It really has to be one of the most frightening predators out there. It's without parallel in the oceans.'

While the giant squid has suckers lined with small teeth on the end of its tentacles, the colossal squid has two rows of rotating sharp hooks, as well as a large beak – a lethal combination. It is believed to eat marine worms, Patagonian toothfish, which themselves reach up to 2.5 metres long, and smaller squid. It finds its prey by lighting up the dark waters.

Adapted from http://pctechtalk.com/topic/40723-deep-sea-discovery-the-monsters-from-the-deep/

1 Notes and planning

What does the passage tell you about the species of colossal squid in general *and* the capture of the creature in New Zealand in particular? Use the space below to plan your answer.

2 Now write a summary of what the passage tells you about the species of colossal squid in general *and* the capture of the creature in New Zealand in particular. You should write no more than 200 words.

Exercise 6

Read the following extract carefully and then answer the questions which follow.

Timbuktu: A living legend

A visit to the semi-mythical African town of Timbuktu proves that real travel is all about the journey and the destination.

Through the heart of Mali, a land-locked nation set inside the jutting rump of West Africa, there is a delta. A flat and impossibly broad body of water tasselled with ribbon islands, which quite obviously has no real business being there. This is the River Niger, a massive blue-green tract pouring itself entirely contrary to logic, away from the Atlantic towards the core of the continent. On the northern bank of this river lies a town, and on the northern border of this town the first dunes of the vast Sahara retract in waves across a distance barely limited by the horizon. It is dawn.

To the west the full moon is still setting – an oily-yellow ball of fat falling into a cauldron of scrub and sand. To the east a sun yet to rise stains the edge of the sky an almost inexplicable shade of crimson. The colour of a parched throat. Then, as the minutes creep by in the stillness and the dull flanks of the town's mud-brick buildings begin to glow in the precious hours before the baking noon, the desert town of Timbuktu comes alive.

Timbuktu has been prefixed so often by the words 'fabled city' it's now been firmly set in the western imagination as somewhere just outside the map – and clinging as it does to the southern edge of the cartographically blank Sahara, the reality isn't actually that different. However, visiting Timbuktu in the 21st century no longer requires an explorer's iron will and an entourage of native Tuareg tribesmen able to navigate the desert by reading the texture of the sand. But it still takes a bit of doing, which for most travellers is what continues to make the journey worthwhile.

Although it was founded in the 12th century, since 22 September 1960, Timbuktu has been squarely centred within the country now known as the Republic of Mali. One of Africa's poorest nations, culturally Mali is undoubtedly one of the continent's richest, and the heart, the soul, and the glue that binds together a country five times larger than the UK, consisting of countless tribal groups and over a dozen separate dialects, is music.

The Timbuktu of today may have changed somewhat since its 15th-century heyday, when its fame as one of the most prosperous trading points in Africa gave rise to the legend of a city sprung from a land of gold. These days the straggling markets and roadside stalls appear to sell an identically limited inventory of sour oranges and grubby sachets of mobile phone top-up cards.

However, Timbuktu still offers more to its visitors than the mere kudos of arriving. As a UNESCO World Heritage site since 1992, the old-town quarter offers ancient mosques built in the region's unique mud-brick style, a vernacular that looks at first glance like the work of some long-extinct species of giant ant.

Of its three mosques, the Djingareiber Mosque, built in 1325, is the oldest and is open to tourists, while the Sankori Mosque once housed the town's university, one of the world's greatest seats of learning during the Middle Ages. On the edge of the town's Casbah, in the concisely named Institut de Hautes Etudes et des Recherches Islamiques Ahmed Baba, some of the twenty thousand of the university's ancient scrolls so far discovered are on display. These days there's also a modest but reasonable array of hotels, hostels and restaurants throughout the town – the medium-priced Hotel Boctou with its bustling terrace restaurant being arguably one of the most popular.

But it's not the mud-brick buildings or their inhabitants that make Timbuktu special. The magic comes from the simple fact it exists at all and the thrill of being there, which combine to create the strange sensation that, now you're actually here, everywhere else in the world is very far away.

Adapted from www.worldtravelguide.net/

3 WRITING SUMMARIES

1 Notes and planning

Give information about Timbuktu through the ages *and* explain the writer's thoughts about the city. Use the space below to plan your answer.

2 Now write a summary of what the passage tells you about Timbuktu through the ages *and* the writer's thoughts about the city. You should write 200–250 words.

....

....

....

....

....

....

....

....

....

Photocopying prohibited   *Cambridge IGCSE™ First Language English Workbook 2nd edition*

Writing compositions

The Directed Writing tasks that you practised earlier allow you both to show your understanding of what someone else has written as well as to demonstrate your own skills as a writer, in particular through argumentative or persuasive writing. Another key writing skill that you should develop is to write something original based on your own imagination or experience in a **descriptive** or **narrative** essay which will be judged only for how effectively you have expressed yourself in writing. When presenting your work, it is important that you cover both content and structure, and style and accuracy.

As a general rule you should write 350–450 words and it is a good idea to keep your response within this limit when you are writing under timed conditions. Writing at too great length will almost certainly lead to a response that is lacking in organisation and contains avoidable errors of expression.

To remind you, here are the assessment objectives for writing:

- articulate experience and express what is thought, felt and imagined

- sequence facts, ideas and opinions

- use a range of appropriate vocabulary

- use register appropriate to audience and context

- make accurate use of spelling, punctuation and grammar.

Structure

An important skill when you are writing compositions is to focus on organising what you write into a coherent sequence so that a reader can clearly follow your train of thought. Remember: whatever you write and for whatever purpose, it is important to keep your readers in mind – they will not be able to fully understand your ideas if your writing is muddled and unplanned. Organising your ideas into logically structured paragraphs that are linked into a coherent whole is of the utmost importance.

The following two exercises will help you to think about structuring a piece of writing.

Key points

You must choose to write *either* a narrative *or* a descriptive piece of writing. When writing an imaginative essay, it is important not to confuse the features of descriptive and narrative writing. In particular, you should avoid including excessive narrative detail when attempting a descriptive task. It is acceptable to use a general narrative structure (for example, a first person description of different aspects of a scene as you, the writer, move from place to place), but the main focus should be descriptive.

You should only write a story in response to a narrative topic. If you attempt a narrative topic, it is vitally important that you plan events carefully before you start to write, and that you keep the time constraints and recommended word limit clearly in mind. Do not try to write a story that is too complicated for the time available.

Exercise 1

The following steps are taken from a recipe describing how to make pancakes, but they are not presented in a logical sequence.

1 Read through the steps and then reorganise them into the correct order.

The correct order is: ....

2 Rewrite the steps as two paragraphs of continuous prose as part of an email to your younger brother, describing how he should cook pancakes for his friends. (You might like to try the recipe yourself as a reward for all your hard work answering the questions in this workbook!)

1 Crack 2 or 3 eggs into a bowl, beat until fluffy. Add the 500 grams of self-raising flour. Do *not* stir mixture at this point.	**6** Enjoy! Try adding butter, peanut butter, syrup, jam, chocolate chips, cookie or candy crumbles or fruit to your pancakes for a different, more exciting flavour. The varieties are endless. These are the most delectable pancakes you will ever taste.
2 Sprinkle a few drops of water onto your pan. If it 'dances', or jumps from the pan with a sizzle, the pan is ready for the batter.	**7** Add the butter and 350 ml of milk to the mix. Stir gently, leaving some small clumps of dry ingredients in the batter. Do not blend until completely smooth. If your batter is smooth, your pancakes will be tough and flat as opposed to fluffy.
3 Cook the other side until golden and then remove. If you want a deeper colour, repeat the steps for another 30 seconds per side until the pancake is done enough for your taste.	**8** Melt 2 tablespoons of butter in a microwave-safe bowl. Make sure that it is completely melted; about 1 minute is sufficient.
4 Heat a frying pan to a medium heat. If you have an initial 'pancake' setting on your stove, use that. Be sure to use non-stick spray, or a pat of butter, so the pancakes won't stick.	**9** Pour about 3 tablespoons to 1/4 cup batter from the tip of a large spoon, or from a pitcher, onto a hot griddle or greased frying pan. The amount you pour will decide the final size of your pancake. It is best to begin with less batter, and then slowly pour more batter into the pan to increase the pancake size.
5 Cook for about 2 minutes or until the pancake is golden. You should see bubbles form and then pop around the edges. When the bubbles at the edge of the batter pop and a hole is left that does not immediately close up, flip the cake gently.	

....

....

....

....

....

....

....

....

....

....

....

....

....

....

....

....

....

....

....

....

....

Exercise 2

Below are seven paragraphs taken from an account of the history of the town of Port Royal in Jamaica as a home for pirates. The paragraphs, however, are out of their original sequence. Read them carefully and then reorganise them. The first and last paragraphs are in the right place; you should rearrange the other five in a logical order.

A logical order is: ....

1 If you go to Jamaica for a vacation you must investigate what is left of the infamous 'lost pirate city' of Port Royal. It was one of the largest coastal towns in the Caribbean in the 17th and 18th centuries.	**5** As the population grew, it became a very wealthy town owing to its sea trade. By the mid-1600s it was said to have over 5000 residents. Sources say there were over 2000 buildings crowded together, some made of brick and up to four storeys tall. Port Royal also soon owned a wicked reputation for the pirates and privateers who frequented its harbour.
2 For a number of years privateering was a legitimate business; captains of privately-owned warships were granted official approval allowing them to attack ships flying enemy flags. Their cargos and the vessels themselves could be seized and sold for a considerable profit. Eventually, in 1684, France, Spain and England signed a treaty which agreed to an end to hostilities in the West Indies. Legal piracy was no more. However, as many captains and crews did not wish to so easily give up their ventures, piracy continued on the blue waters of the Caribbean.	**6** From Port Royal, Jamaica the 'Brotherhood of the Coast' (as pirates were called in those days) sailed out and raided wealthy merchant vessels and the famous Spanish war ships crossing the seas between Europe and the New World.
3 When they returned to their sanctuary, no mortal dared enter Port Royal in pursuit, as it was guarded by four forts. This pirate haven was one of the best defended ports in the world and most feared.	**7** One of the most famous pirates to have his base at Port Royal was Sir Henry Morgan. Many called him 'the Pirate King', as he amassed a great fortune as well as respect from his many sea battles and raiding ventures. However, once he was knighted by the English King, Charles II, he tried to make the region more respectable by attempting to remove the criminals. He began to hunt down his old pirate buddies and hanged them at Gallows Point. It would be at Morgan's hands that the streets of Port Royal and the story of the pirates would forever change. Eventually he was made Governor of Jamaica.
4 In the Golden Days of Pirates it was called 'the richest and wickedest city in the world'. Men of all races and cultures came to this port to trade their treasures and booty, most looted on the high seas from Spanish and British ships.	Adapted from 'The Lost Pirate City of Port Royal Jamaica' on www.humanities360.com/

Vocabulary

One of the most important points to remember when you write is to try to express your meaning as precisely as possible. This requires thinking carefully about the vocabulary that you use, and how your intended meaning can be affected by your choice of words and the associations that different words can have in the minds of your readers.

Exercise 3

The following passage is taken from the opening chapter of Charles Dickens's novel *Bleak House*. It is a description of 19th-century London, which the writer wants to present to his readers as a thoroughly unpleasant city full of fog and mud.

You will notice that certain words that help to convey this impression have been omitted from the passage. As you read through the description, think of your own words to fill the gaps. Once you have done this, compare your version with Dickens's (which is included in the Answers in the teacher's resource) and then try to decide which vocabulary choices are more effective and why. (Note: this exercise will also help in preparing you for answering questions about a writer's use of language.)

As much mud in the streets as if the waters had but newly retired from the face of the earth, and it would not be wonderful to meet a Megalosaurus, forty feet long or so, ... like an elephantine lizard up Holborn Hill. Smoke , ... down from chimney-pots, making a soft black drizzle, with flakes of soot in it as big as full-grown snowflakes—gone into mourning, one might imagine, for the death of the sun. Dogs, ... in mire. Horses, scarcely better; splashed to their very blinkers. Foot passengers, ... one another's umbrellas in a general infection of ill temper, and losing their foot-hold at street-corners, where tens of thousands of other foot passengers have been slipping and sliding since the day broke (if the day ever broke), adding new deposits to the .... of mud, sticking at those points, ... to the pavement, and accumulating at compound interest.

Fog everywhere. Fog up the river, where it flows among green aits [small islands] and meadows; fog down the river, where it .... defiled among the tiers of shipping and the waterside pollutions of a great (and dirty) city. Fog on the Essex marshes, fog on the Kentish heights. Fog .... into the cabooses [ships' kitchens] of collier-brigs; fog lying out on the yards and hovering in the rigging of great ships; fog .... on the gunwales of barges and small boats. Fog in the eyes and throats of ancient Greenwich pensioners, ... by the firesides of their wards; fog in the stem and bowl of the afternoon pipe of the wrathful skipper, down in his close cabin; fog .... pinching the toes and fingers of his shivering little 'prentice boy on deck. Chance people on the bridges .... over the parapets into a nether sky of fog, with fog all round them, as if they were up in a balloon and hanging in the misty clouds.

Gas .... through the fog in divers places in the streets, much as the sun may, from the .... fields, be seen to loom by husbandman and ploughboy. Most of the shops lighted two hours before their time—as the gas seems to know, for it has a .... and .... look.

From *Bleak House* by Charles Dickens

Accuracy of expression

Accuracy in spelling, punctuation and grammar in all your writing is important as errors of this sort can easily result in a reader becoming confused and your intended meaning being lost. The person who marks your examination paper will understand that the pressure of having to write at length under examination conditions will almost certainly mean that all students will make some errors in their writing and the occasional slip will not prevent full marks from being awarded to a very good piece of writing. However, as part of your preparation, it is important that you think carefully about the types of errors that you are prone to make in your expression, and that you do your best to avoid a careless approach that can cause you to make them, especially when you are writing hurriedly and under pressure.

Exercise 4

Here is an extract from a piece of writing by a student. It has been marked by a teacher who has underlined errors of various kinds but has not actually corrected the mistakes. Rewrite the passage, correcting the errors that are indicated. (They are all points that you will have had explained to you in your English lessons during your time at school.)

Lee returned <u>back</u> home late that night; he was tired and <u>laid</u> down on his bed. It had been a <u>tireing</u> day. He had been in the school <u>since</u> five years and as a senior student he had been asked to judge the Junior <u>Pupils</u> debating competition. Lee was looking forward to his <u>roll</u> as a judge. He was determined to remain <u>uninterested</u> throughout the competition. '<u>Its</u> my opportunity to show how sensible I am and to choose <u>whose</u> the best speaker in the Junior School,' he had said to his mother that morning.

The competition had been of a high standard. According to <u>Lees</u> notes, none of those taking part scored less than six marks out of ten. It was very hard to decide who was the winner as none of them deserved to <u>loose</u> and at least three competitors could <u>of been</u> the winners. Lee finally made his decision after much deliberation and gave the name of the winner to the <u>Principle</u> of the school, who then presented the prize.

....

....

....

....

....

....

....

....

....

....

....

....

....

....

....

....

Composition writing exercises

Here is a selection of tasks for you to practise both descriptive and narrative writing. Remember that you should aim to write 350–450 words and you should aim to spend no more than 60–80 minutes writing each answer. You should also try to write each answer in one continuous session. Do not forget that you should spend some of your time thinking about the task you have chosen and making brief notes of your planned content before you start to write. Try to leave yourself some time to proofread what you have written once you have finished and, in particular, to check for the types of errors that you know you have a tendency to make.

A suggested approach to planning your writing has been provided for the first of the descriptive tasks below, as a guide if you wish to use it.

Descriptive tasks

1 Describe the inside of your favourite shop and some of the people who work there.

Possible approach to planning:

- It is probably better to choose a small shop rather than a large store. It is easier to focus on a small place rather than trying to select relevant features from a larger one.

- Where is the shop located? What does it sell?

- The task specifically mentions the *inside* of the shop – do not waste time describing the exterior.

- Is it an old or a new building? What are the first impressions as you enter the shop? Is it usually very busy or is it quiet?

- What is the atmosphere like in the shop? Describe the most striking things that you see, the sounds of the shop and any smells that are special to this place.

- Do not try to describe too many of the people who work there. Two will be sufficient. It would be a good idea to choose two who contrast with each other, for example, young/old; male/female. Describe their personalities as well as their appearance. Remember, the person reading your description is highly unlikely to have been to the shop that you describe, so you are free to make up details to make your description as interesting as you can – as long as the made-up details are believable!

- You need a conclusion; for example, you could reflect on why you particularly like this place and why you think it important for it not to change.

....

....

....

....

....

....

....

....

....

....

....

2 Describe some members of your neighbour's family and the house in which they live.

....

....

....

....

....

....

....

....

....

....

....

....

....

....

....

....

....

3 Write about your last day at your previous school.

....

....

....

....

....

....

....

....

....

....

....

....

....

....

....

....

....

....

....

....

4 Describe a family birthday celebration and some of the people who were present.

5 Write about a place that makes you feel relaxed *and* a place that makes you feel uneasy.

Narrative tasks

1 'I knew that I should not have listened to my friend ...' Write a story that begins or ends with these words.

....

....

....

....

....

....

....

....

....

....

....

....

....

....

....

....

....

2 'The door at the end of the corridor'. Use this as the title of a narrative.

....

....

....

....

....

....

....

....

....

....

....

....

....

....

....

....

....

....

....

3 Write a story in which mistaken identity plays a major part.

4 'The Lost Bag'. Use this as the title of a narrative.

5 'I looked in the mirror and saw ...' Write a story that begins with these words.

Reinforce learning and deepen understanding of the key concepts covered in the syllabus; an ideal course companion or homework book for use throughout the course.

» Develop and strengthen skills and knowledge with a wealth of additional exercises that perfectly supplement the Student's Book.

» Build confidence with extra practice for each lesson to ensure that a topic is thoroughly understood before moving on.

» Consolidate reading comprehension, analysis and evaluation and improve writing skills with practice using a variety of text types and genres.

» Keep track of students' work with ready-to-go write-in exercises.

» Save time with all answers available online in the Online Teacher's Guide.

Use with Cambridge IGCSE® First Language English 4th edition
9781510421318

For over 30 years we have been trusted by Cambridge schools around the world to provide quality support for teaching and learning. For this reason we have been selected by Cambridge Assessment International Education as an official publisher of endorsed material for their syllabuses.

Working for over **30** YEARS WITH Cambridge Assessment International Education

This resource is endorsed by Cambridge Assessment International Education

✓ Provides support for learners for the Cambridge IGCSE and IGCSE (9-1) First Language English syllabuses (0500/0990) for examination from 2020

✓ Has passed Cambridge International's rigorous quality-assurance process

✓ Developed by subject experts

✓ For Cambridge schools worldwide

HODDER EDUCATION
e: education@hachette.co.uk
w: hoddereducation.com

ISBN 978-1-5104-2132-5

MIX
Paper | Supporting responsible forestry
FSC™ C104740